P9-DMJ-861

THE
VICTORIA
LETTERS

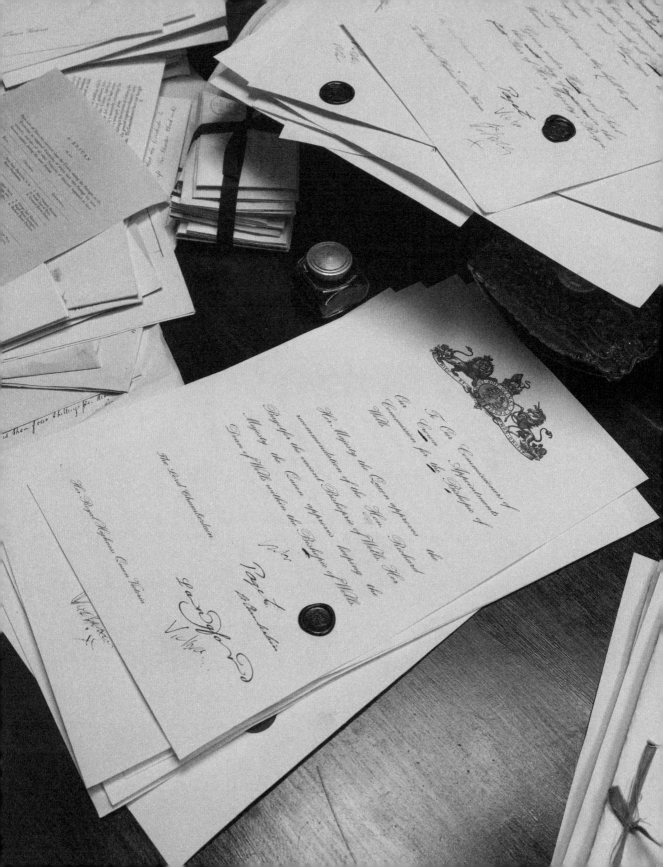

THE
VICTORIA
LETTERS

*The Heart and Mind
of a Young Queen*

Foreword by
DAISY GOODWIN

Written by

HELEN RAPPAPORT

HarperCollins*Publishers*

CONTENTS

FOREWORD

BY DAISY GOODWIN

WHO WAS QUEEN VICTORIA? The image most of us have is of an old lady in a bonnet dressed in black, the woman who is immortalised in countless statues all over the country. Until this year, she was our longest reigning monarch, coming to the throne in 1837 when she was eighteen and reigning for sixty-three years until her death in 1901. Photography was invented in the early years of her reign, but the first images of Victoria and her husband Albert were taken in the 1850s, when Victoria was already a mother of nine, so we have no photographic record of the young Victoria, the teenager who on the morning of 20 June 1837 woke up to find that she was the queen of the most powerful country in the world. But we do have records of her diaries, which have left behind an indelibly vivid picture of the passionate strong-willed girl. Here she is writing about Albert shortly after their engagement, 'I just saw my dearest Albert in his white cashmere breeches, with nothing on underneath!', or after their first parting, 'Oh how I love him, how intensely, how devotedly, how ardently! I cried and felt so sad. Wrote my journal. Walked. Cried.'

I first came across Victoria's journals when I was at university studying nineteenth-century England, and I was immediately taken by the girl that sprang out of the pages. Many years later when I had a teenage daughter of my own, I had a row with her one morning and it suddenly struck me that she was pretty much the same age and size (five foot nothing) as Victoria when she became Queen, and then I thought, what would happen if she woke up one morning and found that she was the most famous woman in the world? From that moment on I started writing scenes in my head, and the idea for *Victoria* the TV series was born.

From the beginning I wanted to show Victoria as a girl who had to do her growing up in public. Most of us get to make our adolescent mistakes in private but Victoria had to do everything under the scrutiny of her courtiers, the press and the public. There were no royal spin doctors in those days, and when Victoria made mistakes, and she made some serious ones in the early years of her reign, there was no press office to hide behind. There were plenty of people who thought that an 18-year-old girl could not be an effective monarch.

But it is clear when you read Victoria's own words that she was a woman with an extraordinary sense of her own identity. Despite having every aspect of her early life controlled by her mother and her mother's advisor Sir John Conroy, Victoria was not moulded by them. From the moment she came to the throne she was determined to do things her way. To take one example, as a baby she had been christened Alexandrina Victoria after her godfather, Alexander of Russia, and her mother Victorine; as a little girl she was called Drina by her mother and her governess Lehzen. But on her accession she decided that instead of taking a 'queenly' name like Mary or Elizabeth, she wanted to be called Queen Victoria – this was shocking at the time because the name Victoria was completely new, but Victoria, my heroine, knew instinctively that it was the right name for her. In that sense at least, she created the Victorian age.

I have used the girl that springs out of Victoria's diaries and letters as the basis for the character that Jenna Coleman plays with such skill in the series. I hope that watching the show will make people curious about Victoria, and this book, so brilliantly put together by the nineteenth-century expert Helen Rappaport, is the perfect place to start if you want to know the history behind the series.

I hope that the series and this book will show that Victoria is very much a heroine for our times. In many ways she is the first woman to have it all – her struggles to be a wife and mother as well as a queen resonate across the centuries. She wasn't perfect but she was brave and resolute and a great deal more than an old lady in a bonnet.

~DAISY GOODWIN, SCREENWRITER OF *VICTORIA*

INTRODUCTION
THE HEART AND MIND OF A YOUNG QUEEN

*'All trades must be learned, and nowadays
the trade of a constitutional Sovereign,
to do it well, is a very difficult one.'*

···· KING LEOPOLD TO QUEEN VICTORIA ····

···· 16 JANUARY 1838 ····

FEW MONARCHS IN BRITISH HISTORY have been so extensively written
about as Queen Victoria. Like Henry VIII and Elizabeth I, it seems that
nothing can dim our enduring fascination with her or our hunger for new
film and TV dramatisations of her life. Much like her two charismatic Tudor
predecessors, Queen Victoria has been the subject of endless interpretation
and re-evaluation, and one might think there is nothing new left to say, no
new revelations to be made.

Until now, most dramatisations have concentrated on the older, more mature
queen, and in particular on her life after Albert, as a widow. But in this new
eight-part series for ITV, screenwriter Daisy Goodwin has put the Queen's very
first faltering steps as monarch under the microscope.

"This book, Mamma gave me"

···· VICTORIA ····

ON 31 JULY 1832, the first page of the story of Victoria's long life was written, when as a 13-year-old princess and already Heir Presumptive to the throne of the United Kingdom of Great Britain and Ireland, she inscribed the flyleaf of the shiny new red leather journal presented to her by her mother:

This book, Mamma gave me, that I might write the journal of my journey to Wales.
~VICTORIA'S JOURNAL, 31 JULY 1832

Over the next 70 years, what began as an educational exercise in recording the relatively mundane events of her young life, to be submitted for daily inspection to her governess and her mother, would grow into 141 handwritten volumes – probably the greatest and most enduring personal record written by any queen at any time in history.

Beginning with her first childish observations of people, places and events, young Princess Victoria recorded a detailed description of her daily life at Kensington Palace, her love for her dolls and her dog Dash; and spoke poignantly of her isolation from the outside world. On her accession in 1837, and moving to Buckingham Palace, she filled the pages of her journals with fascinating accounts of the people who made the greatest impression on her (notably her first prime minister, Lord Melbourne), her hopes and aspirations about the onerous responsibility of becoming Queen that had been thrust upon her very young shoulders, and the joy of finding love and a happy marriage, so rare in the dynastic scheme of things.

In tandem with her diary, Queen Victoria's enormous output of letters dating from 1832 chart a queen in the making and show her wrestling with some of the challenging political issues of her day and making her first difficult decisions as monarch.

This book, in tandem with the television series, tells the touching and intimate developing story of the young princess who became Queen in 1837, based closely on her journals and letters and featuring many key quotations from them. *The Victoria Letters* reveals at first hand a view of the queen who became our second-longest-reigning monarch after Queen Elizabeth II, with all her quirks and foibles, her impetuosity and her compassion.
~HELEN RAPPAPORT, JUNE 2016

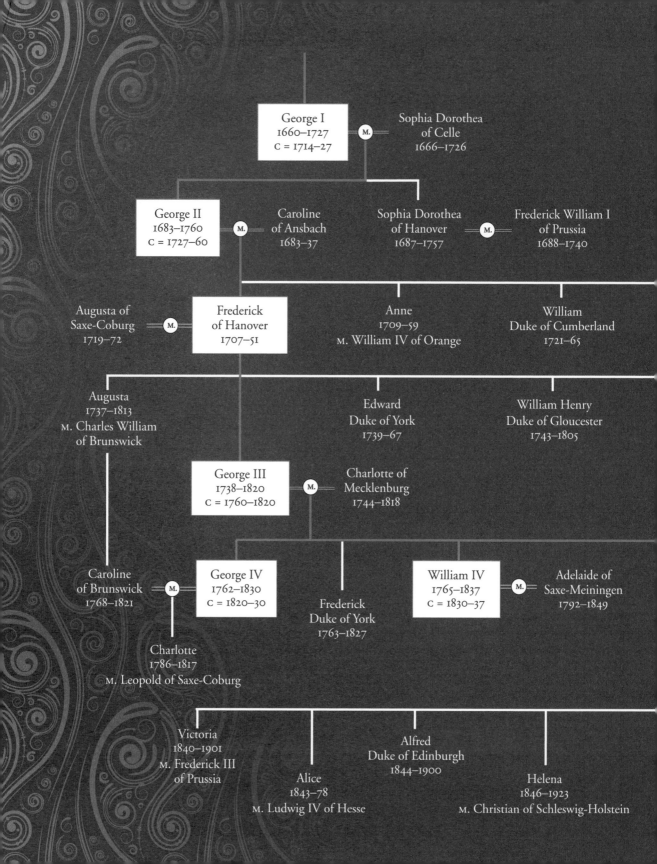

George I
1660–1727
C = 1714–27

M.

Sophia Dorothea
of Celle
1666–1726

George II
1683–1760
C = 1727–60

M.

Caroline
of Ansbach
1683–37

Sophia Dorothea
of Hanover
1687–1757

M.

Frederick William I
of Prussia
1688–1740

Augusta of
Saxe-Coburg
1719–72

M.

Frederick
of Hanover
1707–51

Anne
1709–59
M. William IV of Orange

William
Duke of Cumberland
1721–65

Augusta
1737–1813
M. Charles William
of Brunswick

Edward
Duke of York
1739–67

William Henry
Duke of Gloucester
1743–1805

George III
1738–1820
C = 1760–1820

M.

Charlotte of
Mecklenburg
1744–1818

Caroline
of Brunswick
1768–1821

M.

George IV
1762–1830
C = 1820–30

Frederick
Duke of York
1763–1827

William IV
1765–1837
C = 1830–37

M.

Adelaide of
Saxe-Meiningen
1792–1849

Charlotte
1786–1817
M. Leopold of Saxe-Coburg

Victoria
1840–1901
M. Frederick III
of Prussia

Alice
1843–78
M. Ludwig IV of Hesse

Alfred
Duke of Edinburgh
1844–1900

Helena
1846–1923
M. Christian of Schleswig-Holstein

HOUSE OF HANOVER

FAMILY TREE
1714–1837

Mary
1723–72
M. Frederick II of Hesse-Cassel

Louise
1724–51
M. Frederick V of Denmark

Henry
Duke of Cumberland
1745–90

Caroline Matilda
1751–75
M. Christian VII of Denmark

Edward Duke of Kent
1767–1820
M. Victoria of Saxe-Coburg

Ernest
Duke of Cumberland
1771–1851

Augustus
Duke of Sussex
1773–1843

Adolphus
Duke of Cambridge
1774–1850

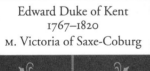

VICTORIA
1819–1901
C =1837–1901

M.

Albert of
Saxe-Coburg & Gotha
1819–61

Alexandra
of Denmark
1844–1925

M.

Edward VII
1841–1910
C = 1901–10

Louise
1848–1939

Arthur
Duke of Connaught
1850–1942

Leopold
Duke of Albany
1853–84

Beatrice
1857–1944
M. Henry of Battenberg

LITTLE DRINA

Dear Mama
A very, very
happy new-year.
Victoria.
1825

'It was a rather melancholy childhood'

···· VICTORIA ····

N 28 APRIL 1819 A RAGGLE-TAGGLE CONVOY of 20 carriages, thick with the dust and grime of 30 days on bumpy roads from Amorbach in Bavaria, rattled up the drive of London's Kensington Palace. The journey its exhausted occupants had just completed – along with a mountain of luggage, two Russian lapdogs and a cage of singing birds – had been a frenetic race against time to ensure that the first legitimate heir to the British throne to be produced by any of George III's sons be born in England.

The soon-to-be parents were Edward, Duke of Kent – the fourth of the nine sons of George III – and his wife, Marie Louise Victoire, formerly a princess of the German duchy of Saxe-Coburg-Saalfeld. They had until now been living at Amorbach in greatly straitened circumstances – thanks to an accumulation of debts brought on by the Duke's compulsive overspending from the moment he completed his military training.

Their one hope of a change in fortunes had followed the death of Princess Charlotte of Wales (the Duke's niece and Duchess's sister-in-law), who had died tragically in 1817. If the Duke outlived his elder, childless brothers, he would become King. And the child his wife was soon to bear, the one most likely to outlive them all, would be fifth in line to the British throne.

By 1819, THE DUKE OF KENT WAS 50. Determined to marry and beget an heir, the previous year he'd discarded his long-term French mistress, Madame St Laurent – giving her a pension for going without making a fuss – and set about finding a wife. As a son of King George III, he knew that his marriage to Victoire of Saxe-Coburg was far from ideal. She was considerably inferior in royal dynastic terms and was a widow with two children. But the Duke needed to legitimise his claim to the throne in the eyes of the public by marrying and becoming a respectable family man.

Despite the draining 427-mile journey from the Continent, at 4.15 a.m. on 24 May, the Duchess of Kent, who seemed to have suffered no adverse effects, gave birth to a pretty, fair and fat baby girl. She was very like her father, having the unmistakably large blue eyes of the Hanoverians. The birth prompted the entire British nation to heave a sigh of relief, for it came during one of the old King George III's bouts of madness and the Regency of his eldest, unpopular son George.

Numb. 17480.

The London

Publiſhed by Au

TUESDAY, MAY 25

Kensington-Palace, May 24, 1819.

THIS morning, at a quarter past four o'clock, the Duchess of Kent was happily delivered of a Princess. His Royal Highness the Duke of Sussex, His Grace the Archbishop of Canterbury, His Grace the Duke of Wellington, Master-General of the Ordnance, the Marquess of Lansdowne, the Earl Bathurst, one of His Majesty's Principal Secretaries of State, the Bishop of London, the Chancellor of the Exchequer, and the Right Honourable George Canning, First Commissioner for the Affairs of India, were in attendance.

Her Royal Highness is, God be praised, as well as can be expected, and the young Princess is in perfect health.

Carlton-House, May 20, 1819.

This day His Royal Highness the Prince Regent, in the name and on the behalf of His Majesty, was

DUCHESS OF KENT:
Driving in a coach from Amorbach, across France, so that you could be born in England – I was so worried that you would come early and your wicked uncles would say you were not English.

....
Top right: Announcement of the Royal birth in *The London Gazette*.
Above: 'Fair and fat' – baby Victoria.

THE DUCHESS OF KENT HAD RESISTED the services of a male physician to deliver her child and had instead brought with her the family's own German obstetrician, Marianne Siebold – one of the first women in Europe to obtain a medical degree. Siebold announced the birth to the dignitaries who had gathered in an ante-room to bear witness to the legitimacy of the birth, among them the Duke of Wellington. 'Boy or girl?' he asked her.

'Girl,' answered the doctor, then added in her thick German accent, 'Ver nice beebee. No big, but full. You know, leetle bone, moosh fat.'

Just three months later, Marianne Siebold would deliver another baby, at the Castle Rosenau near Coburg – the son of the Duchess of Kent's brother, Duke Ernest of Saxe-Coburg, and a cousin to the little Princess. From the outset, the grandmother of the two infants, the dowager Duchess of Saxe-Coburg-Saalfeld, was determined that her dear grandson Albert and her adored new granddaughter should one day marry. From her home in Ebersdorf she wrote adoringly of little baby Albert. 'What a charming pendant he would be to the pretty cousin,' she remarked, setting the matchmaking wheels in motion.

....
Above: Young Prince Albert, Victoria's cousin and young suitor.
Opposite: Princess Charlotte – whose death brought Victoria closer to the throne.

PRINCESS CHARLOTTE

'She might have been saved if she had not beeen so much weakened'

···· V I C T O R I A ····

CHARLOTTE (BORN 1796), only child of George, Prince Regent by his wife Caroline of Brunswick, was until her death George III's only legitimate grandchild. Warm-hearted and engagingly impulsive, she was under pressure to secure an advantageous dynastic union through marriage to Prince William of Orange. She was desperate to find an alternative, and after meeting Leopold of Saxe-Coburg-Saalfeld, pleaded with her father to be allowed to marry him instead. Alexander I of Russia saved the situation by offering his sister Anna to the Prince of Orange, and the Prince Regent allowed Charlotte and Leopold to be married in 1816. It seemed a happy union and was popular with the British public, who were overjoyed at the news of their much-loved princess's pregnancy in 1817.

Charlotte, though robust and healthy, was put on a strict diet and bled mercilessly during pregnancy. After an agonising, protracted two days of labour, made worse by incompetent doctors, on 5 November 1817 she gave birth to a stillborn son but shortly afterwards suffered a haemorrhage, and died of shock and exhaustion. Her death provoked unprecedented public grief: regarded as a national disaster, the simultaneous deaths of two heirs to the British throne presented a potential crisis in the monarchy. There

was now a race to see who, among George III's surviving sons, could produce a legitimate heir to replace Charlotte. Adelaide, wife of the Duke of Clarence (the future William IV), hoped to give birth to an heir, but between 1819 and 1822 lost all four of her babies.

Having lost his wife and child, Leopold made it his life's mission to prepare Victoria for the throne that Charlotte should have occupied.

VICTORIA'S DELIGHTED FATHER PRONOUNCED his new baby daughter 'as plump as a partridge' and was ridiculously proud and protective of her.

'Don't drop her! Don't drop her! You might spoil a queen!' he had told the Bishop of Salisbury when he visited soon after and took the baby awkwardly in his arms. Mindful of his daughter's royal prospects, the Duke announced that he wished her to be named Elizabeth after the great Tudor monarch, but at her christening the Prince Regent instead chose the name Alexandrina, after the baby's godparent Tsar Alexander I of Russia, who had recently been Britain's ally in the war against Napoleon. Then, after some prevarication, and with everyone gathered expectantly around the font, he allowed a second name, Victoire, after her mother. Fondly nicknamed Mai-blühme, or May Blossom, by her German mother and grandmother throughout her early childhood, the princess who would become Queen in 1837 was generally known as Drina.

The first happy months of Drina's life were, however, brought to a sudden end when, in January 1820 while staying by the sea at Sidmouth in Devon, her father caught a chill and died of pneumonia. His last words were to beg God to protect his wife and child.

Although she would never have more than the most distant recall of her father, Victoria later remarked, 'I was always taught to consider myself a soldier's child.' She nursed a somewhat rosy view of her father's long and not altogether distinguished military career, which was to give her a lifelong admiration for the army. But she missed his presence and throughout her life, as if to compensate, she would latch on to a succession of strong father figures.

Six days after the Duke's death, his father King George III also died. In less than a week little baby Drina was propelled a great deal closer to the throne.

....
Above: The Duke of Kent, Victoria's father and fourth son of George III.

A Front View of the ROYAL P...

KENSINGTON PALACE

'My dear old home'

···· VICTORIA ····

THE ORIGINAL KENSINGTON PALACE, built on the western edge of Hyde Park in 1661, was a red-brick Jacobean mansion situated in what was then a beautiful, tranquil park of chestnut and beech trees. It was bought by the royal family in 1689 for King William III, because the damp riverside palace at Whitehall had aggravated his asthma. During William's reign the interior of the house underwent extensive renovations designed by the architect Sir Christopher Wren. Queen Anne loved it so much that in 1704 she added a grand orangery, and George I ordered its beautiful gardens to be laid out in 1723–27 by the landscape gardener William Kent.

Little money, however, was spent on maintaining the exterior fabric of the building and it fell into disuse as a royal residence after the death there of George II in 1760. Once Buckingham House (later Palace) was built in central London, George III preferred to live there and Kensington instead became a home for minor royals. The Duke of Kent had been allocated two floors of apartments in 1798, which he furnished, at considerable expense, with new upholstery, curtains and bed hangings. The new furnishings, however, did little to enhance the dark and gloomy interior, which had long been infested with black beetles and other insects, and the Duke's mounting debts drove him to seek refuge abroad.

By the time Victoria was born, Kensington Palace's only remaining occupant was her rather frightening and eccentric Uncle Sussex. She later recalled:

My earliest recollections are connected with Kensington Palace, where I can remember crawling on a yellow carpet spread out for that purpose – and being told that if I cried and was naughty my Uncle Sussex would hear me and punish me, for which reason I always screamed when I saw him!

VICTORIA'S REMINISCENCES OF HER EARLY
CHILDHOOD, WRITTEN IN 1872

Opposite: Kensington Palace, Victoria's childhood home.

Uncle William and Aunt Adelaide send their love to dear little Victoria with their best wishes on her birthday, and hope that she will now become a very good Girl, being now three years old. Uncle William and Aunt Adelaide also beg little Victoria to give dear Mamma and to dear Sissi a kiss in their name, and to Aunt Augusta, Aunt Mary and Aunt Sophia too, and also to the big Doll. Uncle William and Aunt Adelaide are very sorry to be absent on that day and not to see their dear, dear little Victoria, as they are sure she will be very good and obedient to dear Mamma on that day, and on many, many others. They also hope that dear little Victoria will not forget them and know them again when Uncle and Aunt return.

LETTER FROM THE DUCHESS OF CLARENCE TO VICTORIA, 24 MAY 1822

My dearest Uncle – I wish you many happy returns on your birthday; I very often think of you, and I hope to see you soon again, for I am very fond of you. I see my Aunt Sophia often, who looks very well, and is very well. I use every day your pretty soup-basin. Is it very warm in Italy? It is so mild here, that I go out every day. Mama is tolerable well and am quite well. Your affectionate Niece, Victoria. P.S. I am very angry with you, Uncle, for you have never written to me once since you went, and that is a long while.

LETTER FROM VICTORIA TO LEOPOLD, 25 NOVEMBER 1828

FOR THE MOST PART, life at Kensington Palace was unremittingly quiet and uneventful for the young Victoria:

We lived in a very simple, plain manner; breakfast was at half-past eight, luncheon at half-past one, dinner at seven – to which I came generally (when it was no regular large dinner party) – eating my bread and milk out of a small silver basin. Tea was only allowed as a great treat in later years.

~VICTORIA'S REMINISCENCES OF HER EARLY CHILDHOOD, WRITTEN IN 1872

The Duchess, seeking to protect her precious daughter at Kensington from the pernicious influence of court and her predatory Hanoverian uncles, installed little Drina's chintz-curtained bed on one side of her own. 'I was brought up very simply, never had a room to myself till I was nearly grown up and always slept in my Mother's room till I came to the throne,' Victoria later wrote.

On the other side of the Duchess's bed slept Feodora, her daughter from her previous marriage. With playmates very few and strictly vetted, Drina clung to her adored half-sister. Feodora cosseted her and would often take her into her own bed in the mornings; she liked nothing better than pulling her baby sister along in a hand-carriage in the gardens outside. But with the emphasis so much on Drina, Feodora remained a shadowy figure, a 'timid onlooker', as she herself said, of the life of her far more important half-sister.

Victoria adored her: 'My dearest sister was friend, sister, companion, all to me, we agreed so well together in all our feelings and amusements,' she later wrote. It hurt her that so little attention was paid to dearest Fidi, as she called her. 'Why do all the gentlemen raise their hats to me, and not to Feodora?' she once asked.

MRS JENKINS:
Funny to think she's never slept a night alone or even walked down the stairs without her hand needing holding and now she is Queen.

CATHERINE H. FLEMMING PLAYS THE DUCHESS:
'With all the political manoeuvring around the young Victoria, her mother didn't want her to choose the wrong path. Conroy was guiding [the Duchess] and he was the only one she trusted. The Duchess stayed at court even though she was a complete lone wolf. She was never able to step into the bubble of the English royals. She was always someone on the side watching, as a spy, in order to protect her daughter.'

DUCHESS OF KENT

- VICTORIA'S MOTHER -

'Like having an enemy in the house'

···· VICTORIA ····

THE DUCHESS OF KENT WAS born Marie Louise Victoire, daughter of the Duke of Saxe-Coburg-Saalfeld and his wife Augusta in 1786. She was the sister of Leopold, King of the Belgians, and Ernst I, Duke of Saxe-Coburg Gotha – Prince Albert's father. At the age of seventeen she was married to the Prince of Leiningen, a man 23 years her senior, and had two children by him, Charles in 1804 and Feodora in 1807. Widowed in 1814, she was steered in the direction of the unmarried Duke of Kent by her ambitious brother Leopold, who knew that the Duke was keen to father a legitimate heir to the British throne. Although on paper it was an advantageous royal match for a relatively lowly Saxe-Coburg, the Duchess's brief life with the Duke was plagued by financial insecurity and an endless and repeated flight around Europe from their creditors. When the Duke died unexpectedly in 1820, Victoire was left penniless and socially isolated until Leopold, with his eye on the prize of his niece's accession to the throne, bailed her out with an annuity.

Alienated from the court and King William, who disliked her intensely, the Duchess immured herself and her daughter at Kensington Palace. Her vulnerability, isolated and friendless as she was, laid her open to the domineering influence of the controller of her household, Sir John Conroy, who brought out the worst in her by encouraging her ambitions to become Regent. Aware of this and infuriated by the Duchess's constant demands over precedence, William willed himself to stay alive until his niece Victoria had reached her eighteenth birthday in May 1837.

Once upon the throne, Victoria ruthlessly relegated her mother to a separate suite of rooms and it was only later, thanks to Prince Albert, that mother and daughter were reconciled.

ONCE DRINA REACHED THE AGE OF FOUR, a carefully monitored regime, which became known as the 'Kensington System', was devised for her by the Duchess, on advice from the controller of her household, Sir John Conroy. Conroy had previously served as the Duke of Kent's equerry and since his death had gained a considerable hold over the Duchess and her financial affairs. This system of concerted isolation of the young and impressionable child – and which Drina's governess, Fräulein Louise Lehzen, assisted – was designed to exclude any outside influences that might dilute the little girl's undivided loyalty to her mother and undermine her mother's ambitions for Drina's ascent to the throne and her own regency should this happen before she was eighteen. It was important to Conroy and the Duchess to control Drina's dependence on them and resist any attempts by the King to insist that she, as heir to the throne, live with him at court. But in so doing, they turned a little girl's love into resentment and ultimately hatred.

A daily register of Drina's upbringing was meticulously recorded. After breakfast she would take exercise in the garden, often riding on her donkey or in a small pony cart until ten. For the next two hours

....
Right: A young Victoria.

her mother instructed her, assisted by Lehzen (who had originally been Feodora's governess and was appointed subgoverness to Drina in 1824). 'Dear Boppy' – Mrs Brock, her nurse – provided more plain food for lunch at two, followed by lessons until four, after which Drina went outside again for exercise. Another very plain meal of bread and milk came at seven. Promptly at 9 p.m. she was tucked up in the bed next to her mother's. At all times the child was watched, cosseted and protected from potential harm. She was not even allowed to go up and down stairs without an adult holding her hand.

When little Drina's regular education began, her mother warned her tutor, the Revd. George Davys, 'I fear you will find my little girl very headstrong, but the ladies of the household will spoil her.' The Queen herself later freely admitted her early reluctance in the schoolroom, saying that she 'baffled every attempt to teach me my letters up to five years old – when I consented to learn them by their being written down before me'.

It was Davys's task to teach Drina her alphabet and elocution, and to try and soften the edges of the pronounced German accent she had assimilated from her mother. Feodora also helped with spelling, including the composition of one of the four-and-a-half-year-old's first, very forthright, letters – addressed to the Revd. Davys:

MY DEAR SIR, I DO NOT FORGET MY LETTERS NOR WILL I FORGET YOU ~VICTORIA

Reading was *de rigueur* – mainly the scriptures and a great deal of devotional literature. Her mother allowed some poetry, but very little fiction. Mr Stewart came over from Westminster School to teach Drina writing and arithmetic; Madame Bourdin arrived twice a week to teach dancing and deportment; Mr Bernard Sale from the Chapel Royal encouraged Drina's musical talents and her singing; her riding master Mr Fozard ensured that she became a most accomplished horsewoman, while Richard Westall of the Royal Academy nurtured her considerable talent for painting and sketching, and she was also taught French by M. Grandineau and German by the Revd. Henry Barez; Latin and Italian were added later.

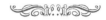
VICTORIA:
There was a time, Mama, when I needed your protection, but instead you allowed Sir John to make you his creature.

MORE IMPORTANTLY PERHAPS in that early training, Drina was taught always to be truthful, punctual and frugal and to take plenty of fresh air and exercise. She went out into Kensington Gardens in all weathers, sometimes on Dickey, her favourite white donkey. Dickey – a present from the Duke of York – its head decorated with blue ribbons, was led by an old soldier who had once served her father. Whenever the little princess emerged from the Palace, often holding hands with Feodora, she was friendly to everyone she met, bidding them 'Good morning' with a smile.

By the age of eleven she seemed exceptionally accomplished and forward for her age. 'A child of great feeling,' thought the Revd. Davys. She was impulsive and generous – but she could also be wilful, and, as the Behaviour Books recording her every misdemeanour noted, on one occasion she had been 'very very very horribly naughty'.

Queen Victoria later explained that 'I was naturally very passionate, but always most contrite afterwards'. She may have been stubborn and impetuous but an abiding quality, from a young age, was her truthfulness, reflected in the often surprisingly candid comments in her journal.

High days and holidays in the protected life of young Drina during the 1820s amounted to summer breaks at Ramsgate and other seaside towns, where she rode her donkey on the sands and was sometimes allowed to play with children of the gentry. Other than this, visits to her mother's brother, Uncle Leopold, were the thing she most longed for. 'Claremont remains as the brightest epoch of my otherwise rather melancholy childhood,' the Queen later wrote, and she and Feodora would often stay at this Palladian mansion near Esher in Surrey for weeks or months at a time, taking great delight in playing in its huge parkland and gardens.

....
Right: Princess Victoria in Kensington Gardens.

Twenty years later her sister recalled in a letter how much the two sisters had loved Claremont in comparison to Kensington Palace – to which they always returned with heavy hearts:

> *When I look back upon those years, which ought to have been the happiest in my life, from fourteen to twenty, I cannot help pitying myself. Not to have enjoyed the pleasures of youth is nothing, but to have been deprived of all intercourse, and not one cheerful thought in that dismal existence of ours, was very hard. My only happy time was going or driving out with you and Lehzen; then I could speak and look as I liked.*
>
> ~LETTER FROM FEODORA, 1843

VICTORIA:
When I was growing up, Mama and Sir John – they kept me under constant supervision. I was allowed no friends, no society, no life of my own.

During this difficult time, Drina's German grandmother, Augusta of Saxe-Coburg-Saalfeld, continued to dote on and adore her little May Blossom from a distance. In 1825 the 68-year-old visited for two months. It was a moment that little Drina had longed for:

> *I recollect the excitement and anxiety I was in, at this event, going down the great flight of steps to meet her when she got out of the carriage, and hearing her say, when she sat down in her room, and fixed her fine clear blue eyes on her little grand-daughter whom she called in her letters: 'The flower of May', 'Ein schönes Kind' – 'a fine child'.*
>
> ~VICTORIA'S REMINISCENCES OF HER EARLY CHILDHOOD,
> WRITTEN IN 1872

....
Left: Princess Augusta, Victoria's grandmother.

She was a good deal bent and walked with a stick, and frequently with her hands on her back. She took long drives in an open carriage and I was frequently sent out with her, which I am sorry to confess I did not like, as, like most children of that age, I preferred running about. She was excessively kind to children, but could not bear naughty ones, and I shall never forget her coming into the room when I had been crying and naughty at my lessons – from the next room but one, where she had been with Mamma – and scolding me severely, which had a very salutary effect.

VICTORIA'S REMINISCENCES OF HER EARLY CHILDHOOD, WRITTEN IN 1872

AUGUSTA WAS BESOTTED WITH her beloved granddaughter, enthusing about her in letters home and proclaiming her to be 'incredibly precocious for her age'. She had never seen 'a more alert and forthcoming child'.

> *Little Mouse is charming: her face is just like her father's, the same artful blue eyes, the same roguish expression when she laughs. She is big and strong as good health itself, friendly and cuddlesome – I would even say obliging – agile, poised, graceful in all her movements. [...] When I speak incorrectly, she says quite softly, 'Grandmama must say…' and then tells me how it should be said. Such natural politeness and attentiveness as that child shows has never come my way before.*
>
> ~LETTER FROM AUGUSTA, 6 AUGUST 1825

Augusta did, however, worry that Drina 'eats a little too much, and almost always a little too fast', and noted that she was also rather short for her age. But she was already displaying other far more important qualities. Grandmama Augusta was one of the first to observe an enduring trait of the future Queen: 'when she enters a room, and greets you by inclining her head, according to the English custom, there is staggering majesty'.

In February 1828 came a terrible wrench for Drina when Feodora, now aged eighteen, left England to marry Ernst, Prince of Hohenlohe-Langenburg – a man much older than herself, whom she hardly knew. From her new home she wrote endless letters to her half-sister in England, filled with love and sorrow at their separation.

If I had wings and could fly like a bird, I should fly in at your window like the little robin to-day, and wish you many very happy returns of the 24th, and tell you how I love you, dearest sister, and how often I think of you and long to see you. I think if I were once with you again I could not leave you so soon. I should wish to stay with you, and what would poor Ernst say if I were to leave him so long? He would perhaps try to fly after me, but I fear he would not get far; he is rather tall and heavy for flying. So you see I have nothing left to do but to write to you, and wish you in this way all possible happiness and joy for this and many, many years to come. I hope you will spend a very merry birthday. How I wish to be with you, dearest Victoire, on that day!

LETTER FROM FEODORA TO VICTORIA, MAY 1829

Georgius D.G. Mag. Britanniæ, Franciæ et Hiberniæ Rex Fidei Defensor

Brun. et Lunen. Dux. S.R.I. Arch. Thefau. et Princeps Elector &c. Jnauguratus XX die Octobris 1714.

Kneller S.R. Imp. et Mag. Brit. Baronet. pinx.   Ab Originali I. Smith Fec. et ex. 1715.

THE HANOVERIANS

*'I am far more proud of my Stuart than
of my Hanoverian ancestors'*

···· VICTORIA ····

B Y BECOMING QUEEN, Victoria ended an uninterrupted line of Hanoverian
kings from 1714 when George I, Elector of Hanover, assumed the British throne
after Queen Anne died childless. To have a young, virginal queen on the throne after
a long line of disreputable males was a refreshing change: the Hanoverians had not
endeared themselves to the British public. Collectively the four Georges and William
preceding Victoria were looked upon, along with their mistresses and scores of illegitimate
children, as rogues, blackguards and fools from a petty provincial German kingdom.
The public baulked at having to support the vast entourage of dependents (including
two mistresses) accompanying George I to England.

His son, George II, provoked a deep, abiding hatred in the Scots when he ordered the
brutal suppression of the Jacobite Rebellion (1745–46).

George III's tumultuous 60-year reign was punctuated by scandal, political disaster and
madness. A devoted husband and father at home, producing fifteen children with his long-
suffering wife Caroline, George lost the American colonies in 1783 and quarrelled endlessly
with his heir, who assumed the Regency in 1811 upon George's last, most crippling descent
into madness.

George IV, a man of considerable aesthetic taste and a patron of the arts, was nevertheless
a lazy spendthrift who abandoned his wife Caroline of Brunswick and squandered a fortune
on his lavish coronation. Despite lingering gossip about the 'bad blood' of the Hanoverians,
Drina had taken a liking to her 'Uncle King', as she referred to George IV on a visit to
Windsor (1826), remembering him as *large and gouty but with a wonderful dignity and
charm of manner'. 'Give me your little paw,'* he said, lifting her into his carriage – a jaunt
that had greatly pleased the young princess.

In contrast, she found the last Hanoverian king, her uncle William IV, *'very odd and
singular',* but appreciated his kindness and determination that she be properly prepared
for a monarch's onerous duties. Although the new Queen's reign would depart dramatically
from the path laid by her royal predecessors, Victoria would carry one heritage with her:
the slightly bulging blue eyes, round face prone to chubbiness and receding chin were all
inherited by her children – unmistakable markers of Victoria's Hanoverian line of descent.

·······
Opposite: George I, first Hanoverian king.

As the 1820s proceeded, Little Drina's own path to the throne became ever more inevitable. Her uncle, the Duke of York, died in 1827, and in June 1830 King George IV died, making Drina now heir presumptive to the throne after her uncle, the new king William IV. It provided Grandmama Augusta with a moment's pause for thought:

> *God bless old England, where my beloved children live, and where the sweet blossom of May may one day reign! May God yet, for many years, keep the weight of a crown from her young head, and let the intelligent, clever child grow up to girlhood before this dangerous grandeur devolves upon her!*
> ~LETTER FROM AUGUSTA TO THE DUCHESS OF KENT, MAY 1830

In the seven years that followed, Little Drina proved to be more than equal to the challenge that lay before her.

FROM KENSINGTON PALACE TO BUCKINGHAM PALACE

My dear Mamma.

I congratulate you on dear Grandmamma's birthday; I hope you will have a very happy day.

your very affectionate Victoria.

Jan: 19th 1828.

'She evinces much talent in whatever she undertakes'

···· DUCHESS OF KENT ····

WHEN PRINCESS VICTORIA was eleven, by now a rather more diligent and conscientious pupil, she is said to have finally discovered that she was in direct line to the throne. Leafing through the pages of a court almanac with her governess Lehzen, she came across a genealogical table of the British succession. Lehzen, writing to Victoria many years later, recalled that the Princess had remarked, 'I never saw that before.'

'It was not thought necessary you should, Princess,' I answered. – 'I see, I am nearer to the Throne, than I thought.' – 'So it is, Madam,' I said. – After some moments the Princess resumed, 'Now, many a child would boast, but they don't know the difficulty; there is much splendour, but there is more responsibility!' The Princess having lifted up the forefinger of Her right hand, while she spoke, gave me that little hand saying, 'I will be good!'

~LETTER FROM LEHZEN TO VICTORIA, 2 DECEMBER 1867

BY THE EARLY 1830S, Victoria was being schooled well beyond her years; training fit for the throne that now, in all likelihood, awaited her. Upon learning of her position as heir presumptive, she is said to have told Lehzen, 'I understand now, why you urged me so much to learn, even Latin.' She was indeed a good Latin scholar – tackling Virgil and Horace – and a fluent linguist.

Undoubtedly one of Victoria's greatest joys in the schoolroom came in 1835, when the Irish-Italian bass baritone Luigi Lablache was appointed to give her singing lessons, in so doing nurturing a lifelong love of Italian opera.

She was still very small for her age – which she worried about – and the Duke of Wellington still found her German accent troubling. Some of Victoria's 'mangled phrases' were, he said, 'particularly unpleasant, coming from the lips of an English princess'. Victoria dissolved into floods of tears when she heard this. Uncle Leopold was also concerned that her love of food was causing her to put on weight. Victoria reassured him, writing from the seaside in 1834: 'I wish you could come here, for many reasons, but also to be an eye-witness of my extreme prudence in eating, which would astonish you.'

I like Lablache very much, he is such a nice, good-natured, good-humoured man, and a very patient and excellent master, he is so merry too (...) I liked my lesson extremely; I only wish I had one every day instead of one every week.

VICTORIA'S JOURNAL, 3 MAY 1836

IN PREPARATION FOR his niece's accession, King William ordered that an English aristocrat, the Duchess of Northumberland, be appointed to work with Lehzen on teaching Victoria court and ceremonial etiquette and training her in deportment and the social graces. But despite this Victoria continued to gravitate ever more to her governess.

Lehzen remained her closest companion, her trusted friend and ally, so much so that Kensington Palace became clearly divided into two camps, with the Duchess and Sir John Conroy in one and Victoria and Lehzen in the other. Although Sir John Conroy's daughter Victoire was brought occasionally to play with her, Victoria spent much of her time alone with her treasured dolls: wooden ones, paper ones, dolls made of leather and expensive wax dolls sent from Berlin – 132 of them in all, carefully organised and listed in her childlike hand in a small copy book. Each doll had its own name, an explanation of which person it represented – if based on a real person – and who made her costume (herself or Baroness Lehzen).

Victoria's favourites were the plain wooden jointed dolls of 3–9 inches long with 'small, sharp noses, and bright vermilion cheeks' that would fit in her dolls' house. She based their costumes on those of real-life actors, opera singers and ballet dancers she admired, sewing tiny ruffles 'with fairy stitches' and making 'wee pockets on aprons embroidered with red silk initials'. The dolls were fitted onto a long board full of pegs by their feet so that Victoria could position them and rehearse court receptions, drawing rooms and levées with them.

When she reached the age of fourteen she packed them all away, but she kept them safely stored in a box even after she came to the throne. Recording one of her first conversations with her future favourite Lord Melbourne, she described how, even then, they 'spoke of my former great love of dolls'.

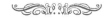

CONROY:
Still playing with dolls,
Your Majesty?

DUCHESS:
You must put away
such childish things
now, Drina. I am afraid
that your carefree
days are over.

**DANIELA HOLTZ PLAYS
BARONESS LEHZEN**

'Lehzen was really Victoria's only confidante and she never betrayed her, never played power games with her. She understood monarchy and power and when Victoria was Queen, she controlled the people who went to her, to protect her.'

BARONESS
LOUISE LEHZEN

*'Dear Lehzen who has
done so much for me'*

···· VICTORIA ····

OUISE LEHZEN, ALONG WITH UNCLE LEOPOLD, was one of the guiding presences in Victoria's early life. One of nine children of a Lutheran pastor, the plain, long-nosed Lehzen had lived in obscurity until the age of 35 when she was appointed governess to the Duchess of Kent's daughter Feodora and brought to England with the family. In service to Victoria from 1824, she rose from subgoverness to friend and adviser and then to lady of the Bedchamber and effective private secretary during those crucial formative years. George IV rewarded her with the honorary title of Hanoverian baroness in 1827 – a title that rather went to Lehzen's head. Her overweening manner thereafter antagonised many members of the household, who resented the lowly-born Lehzen's tyranny. They made cruel jokes about her, among them Lady Flora Hastings, who derided the Baroness's eccentric habit of sprinkling caraway seeds – specially sent over from Hanover – on all her food.

Lehzen was extremely conscientious, to the point of excess, in her duties as governess. Although she could be overly censorious at times, she was also skilful at managing Victoria's legendary tantrums. More importantly, she kept the lonely little girl company and amused her between lessons – their favourite pursuit together being the dressing of Victoria's many dolls.

During her early years Victoria was offered few diversions from the oppressive life at Kensington Place, beyond occasional summer breaks by the sea at Ramsgate and, in 1830, a long holiday to the spa town of Malvern in Worcestershire. En route, she and the Duchess passed through the Midlands where the streets had thronged with people out to greet her. They stopped briefly to see glass-blowing and coining, and visited a porcelain works in Worcester, but otherwise Victoria was not exposed to the realities of Britain's industrial heartland. There was also a visit to Norris Castle on the Isle of Wight in 1833, and that same year, on her fourteenth birthday, Victoria enjoyed her first royal ball:

At half past seven we went with Charles, the Duchess of Northumberland, Lady Catherine Jenkinson, Lehzen, Sir George Anson, and Sir John, to a juvenile ball that was given in honour of my birth-day at St. James's by the King & Queen. We then went into the closet, soon after the doors were opened and the King leading me, went into the ball-room. Madame Bourdin was there as dancing-mistress. Victoire was also there, as well as many other children whom I knew. Dancing began soon after. I danced first with my cousin George Cambridge, then with Prince George Lieven, then with Lord Brook [...] We then went to supper. It was half past 11. The King leading me again. I sat between the King and Queen. We left supper soon. My health was drunk. I then danced one more quadrille with Lord Paget. I danced in all eight quadrilles. We came home at half past 12. I was very much amused. I was soon in bed and asleep.

~VICTORIA'S JOURNAL, 24 MAY 1833

MELBOURNE:
Lady Portman knew your father, Ma'am.

＊＊

LADY PORTMAN:
Such a handsome man, Ma'am. And a very good dancer.

＊＊

VICTORIA:
Was he? I never knew. That must explain why I love dancing so much.

Victoria's singing lessons, occasional visits to the opera and ballet, and the long, vigorous horse rides she enjoyed at a gallop, all contributed to the variety of experience she so craved. But nothing was better than the joy of a visit in 1834 from Feodora and in 1835 from Uncle Leopold and her new aunt Louisa. 'What a happiness it was for me to throw myself in the arms of that dearest of Uncles, who has always been to me like a father, and whom I love so dearly!' she wrote, noting the pleasure of his company at dinner, in contrast to being 'immured' at Kensington: 'I long sadly for some gaiety,' she wrote plaintively.

During this time, the British public began taking a growing interest in its young queen-in-waiting; Victoria, they declared, was something of a prodigy. 'Her powers of attention appear extraordinary for her age, and her memory extremely retentive, which indeed phrenologists would infer from the prominency of her eyes,' noted one observer. Not only was this gifted young mind receiving the best education, but, thanks to Lehzen's firm management, Victoria's volatile temper had also been curbed, for her governess allowed 'no indulgence of wrong dispositions, but corrects everything like resistance, or a spirit of contradiction, such as all children will indulge if they can'.

Meanwhile, Parliament addressed the urgent question of what should happen if the King died before Victoria reached her majority, and decreed that her mother should become Regent, until completion of Victoria's eighteenth year, and in recognition of this the Duchess was granted an extra £10,000 a year, for Victoria's household and education. Although her preposterous demand to be titled 'Dowager Princess of Wales' was thrown out, she was duly grateful: 'This is the first really happy day I have spent since I lost the Duke of Kent,' she said. She was proud of her daughter's progress:

> *She evinces much talent in whatever she undertakes [...] The dear girl is extremely fond of music, she already fingers the piano with some skill, and has an excellent voice.* ~DUCHESS OF KENT

With Victoria now established as heir apparent, the Duchess of Kent, eager to acquire as much prestige for her as possible, orchestrated a series of 'royal progresses' (as King William rather sarcastically called them) to market the Princess to her adoring and curious public. Building on the isolating Kensington System that they had forced Victoria to endure, these excursions were also intended to do the same for the Duchess and Conroy, who harboured ambitions to be regents until Victoria reached the age of 21. A regency would provide them both with considerable wealth, power and status, something they both craved.

CONROY:
Do you really imagine
that you can step from
the schoolroom
straight to the throne
without guidance?

WHEN VICTORIA REACHED thirteen Leopold decided the time was right to prime her for her important future role. She was no longer *a little princess*, he wrote:

> This will make you feel, my dear Love, that you must give your attention more and more to graver matters. By the dispensation of Providence you are destined to fill a most eminent station; to fill it well must now become your study. A good heart and a trusty and honourable character are amongst them of indispensable qualifications for that post.
>
> You will always find in your Uncle that faithful friend which he has proved to you from your earliest infancy, and whenever you feel yourself in want of support or advice, call on him with perfect confidence.
>
> ~LETTER FROM LEOPOLD TO VICTORIA, 22 MAY 1832

In 1834 at the end of another tour, first in Kent round the stately homes at Knole and Penshurst and then to the north to visit York, Belvoir Castle and attend the races at Doncaster, Victoria wrote a warm letter to Uncle Leopold, who in 1832 had finally remarried:

My dearest Uncle – Allow me to write you a few words, to express how thankful I am for the very kind letter you wrote me. It made me, though, very sad to think that all our hopes of seeing you, which we cherished so long, this year, were over. I had so hoped and wished to have seen you again, my beloved Uncle, and to have made dearest Aunt Louisa's acquaintance. I am delighted to hear that dear Aunt has benefited from the sea air and bathing. We had a very pretty party to Hever Castle yesterday, which perhaps you remember, where Anne Boleyn used to live, before she lost her head. We drove there, and rode home. It was a most beautiful day. We have very good accounts from dear Feodore, who will, by this time, be at Langenburg.

Believe me always, my dearest Uncle, your very affectionate and dutiful Niece,

Victoria.

LETTER FROM VICTORIA TO LEOPOLD, 14 SEPTEMBER 1834

PAUL RHYS PLAYS SIR JOHN CONROY

'He was a self-made, ambitious man. To have got to that position of power in that time, coming from his background, was remarkable and speaks volumes for the intelligence of the man.

He was very loyal to the Duchess, who was constantly being marginalised, and he wanted her to have more power and title so he fought really hard for her. He was a fighter, a proper scrapper, and if it had been in a different direction it could have been for the greater good.'

SIR JOHN CONROY

- CONTROLLER OF THE DUCHESS'S HOUSEHOLD -

'The monster and demon incarnate'

···· VICTORIA ····

SIR JOHN CONROY, BORN IN 1786, was to dominate Princess Victoria's early life. A handsome Irishman, he was appointed equerry to the Duke of Kent in 1818, and rapidly ingratiated himself with the Duchess after the Duke's death, taking control of her affairs. King William despised his blatant ambition and referred to him as 'King John', for Conroy had long nursed delusions of his own, unproven, royal connections. He spent his life aspiring to elevation into the British aristocracy: promotion to a Knight Commander of the Hanoverian Order by George IV had done little to satisfy those ambitions. With the Duchess under his control, he had a major influence over the creation of the Kensington System that isolated Princess Victoria from any unwanted external influences. Power went to his head and he strutted around Kensington Palace as though it were his own private fiefdom.

Conroy's manner towards the Duchess was frequently overbearing and at times openly and worryingly seductive. It crossed the bounds of propriety and set tongues wagging, to the point where some even alleged that Victoria was his child and not the Duke's. There is nothing to support this claim, but Conroy certainly took advantage of the Duchess's weakness and vulnerability, exerting a pernicious influence over her that the young Victoria absolutely despised.

N 31 JULY 1832, on the eve of a three-month trip to Wales, Victoria excitedly contemplated the clean white pages of the brand new journal that her mother had given her. On the following day, she dutifully noted that 'we had left K.P. At 6 minutes past 7' and marked down the precise times and places where they had changed horses along the way: Barnet, St Alban's, Dunstable, Stony Stratford. The road was dusty and it started to rain but she enjoyed every minute of this new adventure and the fact that the carriage went 'at a tremendous rate'.

Throughout her journey Victoria painstakingly entered the details of their itinerary, the visits to Powis and Beaumaris Castles and the return home via Anglesey and the Midlands. Wolverhampton, she noted, was 'a large and dirty town', where she was nevertheless received 'with great friendliness and pleasure'. A pause in heavy rain at Birmingham to change horses provided her with her first sight of the grim conditions in the manufacturing districts:

> We just passed through a town where all coal mines are and you see the fire glimmer at a distance in the engines in many places. The men, women, children, country and houses are all black. But I can not by any description give an idea of its strange and extraordinary appearance. The country is very desolate everywhere; there are coals about, and the grass is quite blasted and black […] every where, smoking and burning coal heaps, intermingled with wretched huts and carts and little ragged children.
>
> ~VICTORIA'S JOURNAL, 2 AUGUST 1832

Soon, however, she was entranced by the more prepossessing splendours of the great country houses: Chatsworth – 'It would take me days, were I to describe minutely the whole' – Hardwick Hall, Shugborough Hall, Alton Towers and Wytham Abbey.

By 1835 the exhausting annual tours had taken a toll on Victoria, bringing her to the brink of physical collapse. Hours and hours of being jolted mercilessly along country lanes and potholed roads gave her headaches and backache. She suffered from travel sickness and in September, after another gruelling tour – of the Midlands, North Country and Norfolk – she became so run down that at Ramsgate she fell seriously ill with typhoid and took to her bed for five weeks. She was devotedly nursed back to health by Lehzen, who insisted on the seriousness of Victoria's illness and that the doctors be called in.

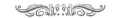

DUCHESS OF KENT:
When she was just a little girl she would show me her journal every night, so I would know everything she was thinking and feeling.

By 1837 Victoria had matured considerably. For the last two years she had been engaged in a detailed correspondence with Uncle Leopold, in which she confidently discussed the intricacies of constitutional history, the workings of the British parliament, and world politics (not to mention enjoying a good gossip about all the family feuding and intrigue in the royal houses of Europe). Her letters to him demonstrate a precocious self-confidence and a lively interest in the workings of Parliament:

> You may depend upon it that I shall profit by your excellent advice respecting Politics. Pray, dear Uncle, have you read Lord Palmerston's speech concerning the Spanish affairs, which he delivered the night of the division on Sir Henry Hardinge's motion? It is much admired. The Irish Tithes question came on last night in the House of Commons, and I am very anxious for the morning papers to see what has been done.
>
> ~LETTER FROM VICTORIA TO LEOPOLD, 2 MAY 1837

On 24 May 1837 Victoria celebrated her eighteenth birthday and a public holiday was declared in Britain. King William sent her a splendid new grand piano as a birthday gift, Kensington Palace was decorated with bunting and the Princess awoke to a chorus of voices serenading her in the garden outside. She did not fail to note the significance of that day in her journal:

> How old! And yet how far am I from being what I should be. I shall from this day take the firm resolution to study with renewed assiduity, to keep my attention always well fixed on whatever I am about, and to strive to become every day less trifling and more fit for what, if Heaven wills it, I'm some day to be.
>
> ~VICTORIA'S JOURNAL, 24 MAY 1837

The courtyard and the streets were crammed when we went to the Ball, and the anxiety of the people to see poor stupid me was very great, and I must say I am quite touched by it, and feel proud which I always have done of my country and of the English Nation.'

VICTORIA'S JOURNAL, 24 MAY 1837

26th May 1837

... The demonstrations of affection and kindness from all sides towards me on my birthday, were most gratifying. The parks and streets were crowded all day as though something very extraordinary had happened. Yesterday I received twenty-two Addresses from various places, all very pretty and loyal; one in particular was very well written which was presented by Mr. Attwood from the Political Union at Birmingham.

LETTER FROM VICTORIA TO LEOPOLD, 26 MAY 1837

I trust to God that my life may be spared for nine months longer. I should then have the satisfaction of leaving the exercise of the Royal authority to the personal authority of that young lady (Victoria), heiress presumptive to the Crown, and not in the hands of a person now near me (the Duchess), who is surrounded by evil advisers and is herself incompetent to act with propriety in the situation in which she would be placed.

PUBLIC SPEECH BY KING WILLIAM AT STATE BANQUET, AUGUST 1836

17th June 1837

My Beloved Child,

… I shall today enter on the subject of what is to be done when King ceases to live. The moment you get official communication of it, you will entrust Lord Melbourne with the office of retaining the present Administration as your ministers. You will do this in that honest and kind way which is quite your own, and say some kind things on the subject. The fact is that the present Ministers are those who will serve you personally with the greatest sincerity and, I trust, attachment. For them, as well as for the Liberals at large, you are the only Sovereign that offers them des chances d'existence et de durée. With the exception of the Duke of Sussex, there is no one in the family that offers them anything like what they can reasonably hope from you, and your immediate successor, with the mustaches (The Duke of Cumberland), is enough to frighten them into the most violent attachment for you … The irksome position in which you have lived will have the merit to have given you the habit of discretion and prudence, as in your position you never can have too much of either…

LETTER FROM LEOPOLD TO VICTORIA, 17 JUNE 1837

THAT EVENING A SPECIAL ball was held for her at St James's Palace, at which, for the first time, Victoria took precedence over her mother. King William had lived long enough to see Victoria reach her majority and, while Conroy and her mother's hopes for a regency were not yet at an end, in Victoria's eyes they most certainly were.

Events soon overshadowed those happy celebrations. By early June it was clear that the King was dying. Victoria wrote to Uncle Leopold:

The King's state, I may fairly say, is hopeless; he may perhaps linger a few days, but he cannot recover ultimately. [...] Poor old man! I feel sorry for him; he was always personally so kind to me, and I should be ungrateful and devoid of feeling if I did not remember this.

I look forward to the event which it seems is likely to occur soon, with calmness and quietness. I am not alarmed at it, and yet I do not suppose myself quite equal to all; I trust, however, that with good-will, honesty and courage I shall not, at all events, fail.

~LETTER FROM VICTORIA TO LEOPOLD, 19 JUNE 1837

William IV died in the early hours of 20 June, bitter that his young heir had so determinedly been kept away from his court – 'at which she ought always to have been present' – by her mother, but relieved that he had protected the throne for Victoria from the 'evil advisers' who surrounded her. Victoria recalled that momentous day in her journal:

I was awoke at 6 o'clock by Mamma, who told me that the Archbishop of Canterbury and Lord Conyngham were here, and wished to see me. I got out of bed and went into my sittingroom (only in my dressing-gown) and alone, and saw them. Lord Conyngham (the Lord Chamberlain) then acquainted me that my poor Uncle, the King, was no more, and had expired at 12 minutes past 2 this morning, and consequently that I am Queen. Lord Conyngham knelt down and kissed my hand at the same time delivering to me the official announcement of the poor King's demise.

~VICTORIA'S JOURNAL, 20 JUNE 1837

....
Right: William IV; on his death Victoria became Queen.

LEHZEN‡
Drina, the messenger is here. With a black armband.

PLAYER'S CIGARETTES

WILLIAM IV

LATER THAT SAME DAY, Victoria met her Privy Council for the first time – alone. When her uncles came forward to pay homage, she managed 'with admirable grace' to prevent them from kneeling to her. In a quivering voice she acknowledged the challenge facing her:

> *This awful responsibility is imposed upon me so suddenly and at so early a period of my life, that I should feel myself utterly oppressed by the burden, were I not sustained by the hope, that Divine Providence, which has called me to this work, will give me strength for the performance of it, and that I shall find in the purity of my intentions and in my zeal for the public welfare that support & those resources that belong to a more mature age and to longer experience.*
>
> ~VICTORIA'S SPEECH TO THE PRIVY COUNCIL, 20 JUNE 1837

Britain seemed, overnight, transformed by the arrival on the throne of a young, untainted queen after a century of Hanoverian males. 'Now everyone is run mad with loyalty to the young Queen,' wrote Sallie Stevenson, wife of the American Ambassador. 'She seems to have turned the heads of the young & old, & it is amazing to hear those grave & dignified ministers of state talking of her as a thing not only to be admired but to be adored.'

From his home in Saxe-Coburg, Victoria's young cousin Albert sent his congratulations:

> *Now you are queen of the mightiest land in Europe; in your hand lies the happiness of millions. May Heaven assist you and strengthen you with its strength in that high but difficult task.*
>
> ~LETTER FROM ALBERT TO VICTORIA, 26 JUNE 1837

VICTORIA:
I intend to see all my ministers alone.

CONROY:
This is not a game. In future you must be accompanied by your mother or me.

DUCHESS:
Yes, Drina, you are just a little girl, you must have advisers.

VICTORIA:
Oh, don't worry, Mamma, I won't be completely alone. I have Dash.

I dressed dear little sweet Dash for the second time after dinner in a scarlet jacket and blue trowers.

VICTORIA'S JOURNAL,
23 APRIL 1833

DASH
VICTORIA'S SPANIEL

'Little Dash is perfection'

···· V I C T O R I A ····

I
N JANUARY 1833 SIR JOHN CONROY presented the Duchess of Kent with a little tricolour Cavalier King Charles Spaniel named Dash. Although the dog initially seemed very attached to her mother, Victoria quickly commandeered it. Within a month it was accepted that he was her dog, supplanting both the dolls and Lehzen as her dearest companion.

'Dear little Dash is a most amusing, playful, attached and sweet little dog. He is so clever also,' she wrote in her journal. She dressed him in a scarlet jacket and blue trousers and at Christmas that year gave him gingerbread and three rubber balls as presents. When she became Queen, Victoria worried about how Dash would settle in at Buckingham Palace but soon recorded in her journal that he 'seemed quite happy in the garden'.

Once word got out that the Queen had a pet dog, many other dogs were offered as gifts. 'You'll be smothered with dogs,' her favourite prime minister, Lord Melbourne, told her. And indeed Victoria was later to own a number of pet dogs: Waldman the dachshund, Islay the terrier, Sharp the collie, and there was, of course, Albert's beloved greyhound Eos. But Dash was the Queen's first and best-loved dog.

It was Albert who broke the news of his death to a heartbroken Victoria: 'I was so fond of the poor little fellow, & he was so attached to me.' She had him buried on the slopes of Windsor Castle near her summer house, and wrote a most touching epitaph:

Here lies Dash, the favourite spaniel of Her Majesty Queen Victoria, by whose command this memorial was erected. He died on the 20th December 1840 in his ninth year. His attachment was without selfishness, his playfulness without malice, his fidelity without deceit. Reader, if you would live beloved and die regretted, profit by the example of Dash.

VICTORIA'S FIRST ACT AS QUEEN was to give her assent to 40 new Bills. On a more personal level, that very first day, she had her bed removed from her mother's room. She ordered the transfer of her household to Buckingham House – which she later renamed Palace, even though it was only half furnished and the carpets not down. Workmen were still busy day and night, and even the bronze entrance gates had not yet been fixed in position. She would miss Kensington Palace, writing:

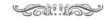

VICTORIA:
But I don't understand
why this is called a
House and not a Palace.
✲✲
MELBOURNE:
You can call it whatever
you want, Ma'am.

> *Though I rejoice to go into B.P. for many reasons, it is not without feelings of regret that I shall bid adieu for ever (that is to say, for ever as a dwelling), to this my birth-place, where I have been born and bred, and to which I am really attached!*
>
> *I have seen my dear sister married here, I have seen many of my dear relations here, I have had pleasant balls and delicious concerts here, my present rooms upstairs are really very pleasant, comfortable and pretty ... I have gone through painful and disagreeable scenes here, 'tis true, but still I am fond of the poor old Palace.*
>
> ~VICTORIA'S JOURNAL, 13 JULY 1837

But for Victoria it was an important moment of transition. Propriety may have demanded that her mother stay with her until she married, but the needy, lonely Little Drina was no more. On 13 July 1837 the Queen left Kensington for what was referred to as 'the New Palace at Pimlico'. She was Queen Victoria now, and in future the Duchess would not enter her rooms unless specifically invited.

THE
MAIDEN
QUEEN

Château de Windsor.
6 7bre 1844. —

... of London ...
complete ...

... the Duke of
Wellington was cheered ...

'How proud I felt to be the Queen of such a nation'

···· VICTORIA ····

ON THURSDAY, 28 JUNE 1838, the whole of London was buzzing with excitement. From seven o'clock that morning a distinguished array of 10,000 lords and ladies, VIPs and diplomats began taking up their places in the specially constructed temporary galleries inside Westminster Abbey, weighed down in their ceremonial robes, plumes and coronets, and bristling with diamonds.

The city hummed with excitement and expectation, as the diarist Lord Greville recorded:

> *The uproar, the confusion, the crowd, the noise are indescribable. Horsemen, footmen, carriages. Squeezed, jammed, intermingled, the pavement blocked up with timbers, hammering and knocking and falling fragments stunning the ears and threatening the head; not a mob here and there, but the town all mob, thronging, bustling, gaping and gazing at everything, at anything, or at nothing; the Park one vast encampment, with banners floating on the tops of the tents, and still the roads are covered, the railroads loaded with arriving multitudes.*
> ~CHARLES GREVILLE'S JOURNAL, 27 JUNE 1838

The masses had gathered to see the new young Queen crowned, and though they did not know it yet, she would be their sovereign for the next 63 years.

S HORTLY BEFORE HER ACCESSION, there were two pressing issues that Victoria had wished to settle. The first was the name under which she would rule as Queen. In anticipation of this, she had written to Uncle Leopold in November 1836:

You are aware, I believe, that about a year after the accession of the present King there was a desire to change my favourite and dear name Victoria to that of Charlotte, also most dear, to which the King willingly consented. On its being told me, I said nothing, though I felt grieved beyond measure at the thought of any change. Not long after this, Lord Grey, and also the Archbishop of Canterbury, acquainted Mamma that the country, having been accustomed to hear me called Victoria, had become used to it, liked it, and therefore, to my great delight, the idea of a change was given up.

~LETTER FROM VICTORIA TO LEOPOLD, 21 NOVEMBER 1836

CONROY:
I suppose the first thing to decide is how you will style yourself. 'Alexandrina' is too foreign and 'Victoria' is hardly a name for a queen. You need something traditional like Elizabeth perhaps, or Anne. Elizabeth the Second sounds very well.

....
Right: An invitation to Victoria's Coronation at Westminster Abbey.

THE SECOND, AND INCREASINGLY URGENT, problem was a much more delicate one. Despite settling into Buckingham Palace with great confidence and spreading her wings, alone, in her own apartments, Victoria had a continuing preoccupation: what to do with Mother?

Her most trusted confidant during this time was her prime minister, William Lamb, 2nd Viscount Melbourne, and she remarked to him, 'How dreadful it was to have the prospect of torment for many years by Mama's living here.' She and the Duchess were not getting on at all. Mama's humour was 'so variable', Victoria complained to him; she was 'touchy and jealous'. She knew that the situation would not change until she married.

'Well then,' replied Lord Melbourne, 'there's *that* way of settling it.' Victoria was appalled. She had absolutely no intention of getting married yet. Here she was, free at last, enjoying the attention and the indulgence that her position brought, and – had she but admitted it – the power too. Why burden herself with all that marriage entailed?

LEHZEN:
How are you finding the north wing, your Royal Highness?

❋

DUCHESS:
Where are my daughter's rooms?

❋

LEHZEN:
In the south wing, Ma'am.

❋

DUCHESS:
And where do you sleep, Baroness?

❋

LEHZEN:
I have a room next to the Queen, with an interconnecting door.

I said to him (Lord M) that I had had a great set to, with Ma (...) that Ma and I had quarrelled about him; that she said Lord M came too often to me; upon which Lord M said: The Duke of Wellington said that was right; and that if he was me, he would establish himself in the Palace,' which I said I wished he would. Then I said, Ma said that Lord M's manners towards me were not good (for they happen to be the admiration of every one – so respectful, yet so fatherly) – which greatly shocked Lord M. 'How can she say that?' he said. I told him that we had also quarrelled about J. C. (John Conroy), and that I had told her that if I ever told her anything, she always repeated it again.

VICTORIA'S JOURNAL, 12 MAY 1839

CONROY:
You never could
take champagne,
Ma'am. I did warn you.
I suggest that you
retire before you
embarrass yourself.

SINCE COMING TO THE THRONE Victoria had quickly made up for the years of seclusion and oppression at Kensington. As Queen, she now had a daily routine that suited herself, and not one dictated by Conroy and her mother. After breakfast at 8 a.m., she received Lord Melbourne in her private boudoir to read and discuss the day's dispatches and deal with other state business. Later in the morning she would receive other cabinet ministers.

After lunch she regularly went out for a vigorous ride attended by her suite and, of course, Lord M. If there was time, she would continue to work on her dispatches. Dinner, at which her mother joined her by invitation, was at 8 p.m., followed by music, card games and conversation with Lord M.

Victoria also held a succession of dinner parties, balls and receptions at Buckingham Palace and Windsor. She revelled in staying up late and dancing till four in the morning. Even on quiet evenings at home, she frequently commented on a weary Lord M's presence until nearly midnight. While she adored every minute of his company and conversation, Victoria's prime minister had to muster all his legendary tact and tolerance to keep up with her youthful energy.

In November 1837 Victoria had attended her first State Opening of Parliament in all her regalia, demonstrating incredible composure in the way she read her speeches in a slow, serious and clear-cut manner. And her newfound position and annual income on the Civil List enabled her at long last to pay off all her father's debts at a stroke.

Victoria was finally free, and she wasn't yet ready to give up her independence through marriage.

As her new reign progressed, so too did preparations for the Coronation. Something approaching 500,000 people had poured into the capital from all over Britain for the occasion; others came from as far away as the USA. The streets were festooned with bunting and every window, balcony or vantage point along the route of the Coronation procession – which Victoria had specifically requested – was filled with spectators, some of whom had paid a considerable price for the privilege. Those too poor to pay for accommodation camped out on the streets and parks overnight.

On 28 June, Victoria was woken at 4 a.m. by the guns in nearby St James's Park going off and 'could not get much sleep afterwards on account of the noise of the people, bands etc'. She was delighted that Feodora had been able to come over for the Coronation, with her husband and two young children. Her sister was in fact the first person to see the Queen on the morning of the Coronation when she came in to admire her gown after breakfast. Uncle Leopold, however, declined the invitation to attend: 'A King and Queen at your dear Coronation might perhaps be a Hors-d'oeuvre,' he told her. It was Victoria's day and he didn't want to upstage it.

Her state procession from Buckingham Palace set off at 10 a.m., wending its way slowly through the crowded streets. She was thrilled by:

> … the millions of my loyal subjects, who were assembled in every spot to witness the procession. Their good humour and excessive loyalty was beyond everything, and I really cannot say how proud I feel to be the Queen of such a nation.
>
> ~VICTORIA'S JOURNAL, 28 JUNE 1838

LEHZEN:
Majesty, it is still so early. You should rest.

VICTORIA:
I can't sleep any longer. I am ready for this day.

DUCHESS OF KENT: No one thought that one day she would be Queen, apart from me.

A GREAT CRY OF 'VIVAT VICTORIA REGINA!' and a flourish of trumpets greeted her as she entered the Abbey, 'looking like a girl on her birthday', as one visitor recalled. In the midst of so much splendour, wearing a vast crimson velvet train carried by eight maids in waiting, Victoria seemed so small and childlike. There had been no proper rehearsal and some of the procedure was bungled, but during the four-and-a-half-hour ceremony she held her nerve. The crown she wore was not the old 7-lb one worn by her predecessors but a much smaller one that had been made specially for her, but which nevertheless gave her a headache by the end of the day. When it came to her crowning, the Duchess of Cleveland recalled:

> *I think her heart fluttered a little as we reached the throne; at least, the colour mounted to her cheeks, brow, and even neck, and her breath came quickly. However, the slight emotion she showed was very transient, and she stood perfectly motionless while the Archbishop, in an almost inaudible voice, proclaimed her our undoubted Sovereign and Liege Lady.*
>
> ~RECOLLECTIONS OF THE DUCHESS OF CLEVELAND

Despite it having been an exhausting day for her, Victoria described the ceremony in detail in her journal. At the moment the crown was placed on her head she recalled:

> *My excellent Lord Melbourne, who stood very close to me throughout the whole ceremony, was completely overcome at this moment, and very much affected; he gave me such a kind, and I may say fatherly look. The shouts, which were very great, the drums, the trumpets, the firing of the guns, all at the same instant, rendered the spectacle most imposing.*
>
> ~VICTORIA'S JOURNAL, 28 JUNE 1838

Outside, a tremendous crowd thronged Hyde Park, where a huge fair was in full swing, as Victoria made her way back to the Palace. She was intensely relieved at having acquitted herself well. It was only when she was safely inside that the child in her resurfaced, when she heard Dash bark. There and then, and still in her ceremonial garments, she swept him up in her arms and took him off for a bath.

See overleaf: Front page of the *Observer* on Coronation day, 28 June 1838.

N THE EVENING OF HER CORONATION the Queen entertained 100 guests to dinner at Buckingham Palace.

I said to Lord Melbourne when I first sat down that I felt a little tired on my feet; 'You must be very tired,' he said. Spoke of the weight of the Robes, etc., etc., the Coronets; and he turned round to me with the tears in his eyes, and said so kindly: 'And you did it beautifully – every part of it, with so much taste; it's a thing that you can't give a person advice upon; it must be left to a person.' To hear this, from this kind impartial friend, gave me great and real pleasure.

~VICTORIA'S JOURNAL, 28 JUNE 1838

Meanwhile, London was aglow with illuminated decorations displaying the initials VR, royal crowns and stars, and two huge firework displays were in full swing in Green Park and Hyde Park. Many of the theatres – at Victoria's express command – threw their doors open for free and there were Coronation dinners up and down the land.

The Coronation expenses, later announced at £69,421, proved to be a snip compared to the enormous £238,000 costs incurred by George IV for his lavish ceremony in 1821, and William IV's had also been four times the cost of Victoria's. Yet not everyone was happy about this, with some proclaiming Victoria's to be 'A Penny Coronation', lacking the pomp and pageantry that was her due. It was, nevertheless, the first occasion when the British people had enjoyed the novelty of seeing a young and pretty queen crowned. The last female monarch, Queen Anne, who was rheumatic and overweight, had been unable to walk or stand for long during her own coronation in 1702.

MELBOURNE:
The Queen is
a remarkable young
woman and I consider
it the greatest privilege
of my career to
serve her.

THE CORONATION OF QUEEN VICTORIA.

....
Opposite: Victoria, crowned while still in her teens.
Right: The Coronation of Queen Victoria.

Even as the euphoria of the Coronation lingered and Victoria continued to bask in the full force of public affection, she was to have a rude awakening: her first experience of the difficult path a monarch must tread in order to retain that fragile approval would teach her a very painful personal lesson. And it was provoked by the long-simmering hostilities between her own entourage and that of her mother.

Victoria's longstanding dislike of Sir John Conroy had by no means diminished on her accession. He had envisioned himself as her Private Secretary, but she gave the idea short shrift, as she told her mother:

I thought you would not expect me to invite Sir John Conroy after his conduct towards me for some years past, and still more so after the unaccountable manner in which he behaved towards me, a short while before I came to the Throne.

~LETTER FROM VICTORIA TO THE DUCHESS OF KENT, 17 AUGUST 1837

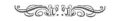

CUMBERLAND:
The Queen must
be held to account.
She has treated
Lady Flora quite
shamefully.

When it came to Conroy, the young queen was ruthless. She had always hated his rude, peremptory manner, his habit of barging into her rooms unannounced and his predatory and avaricious behaviour. And no one was surprised when it was later shown that he had siphoned off £60,000 of her mother's money.

Although on her accession she had banished Sir John from her apartments, he still attended the Duchess in hers. He was regularly seen there in the company of the Duchess's favourite lady in waiting and confidante, Lady Flora Hastings. In January 1839, on a visit to Scotland, Lady Flora travelled with the 53-year-old Sir John. Not long after her return, her abdomen appeared to be distended – a fact that did not pass unnoticed when in the Queen's presence. Victoria and Lehzen both agreed 'how exceedingly suspicious her figure looked'. In conversation with two of her ladies of the Bedchamber, Lady Portman and Lady Tavistock, Victoria concluded that Lady Flora was pregnant. She was horrified. 'The Honour of the Queen's Household' was being called into question, with Sir John Conroy assumed culprit.

2 February 1839

Lady Flora had not been above two days in the house, before Lehzen and I discovered how exceedingly suspicious her figure looked. More have since observed this, and we have no doubt that she is – to use the plain words – with child!! Clark cannot deny the suspicion; the horrid cause of all this is the Monster and demon Incarnate (Conroy) whose name I forbear to mention.

Lady Tavistock accordingly with Lehzen's concurrence told Lord Melbourne of it, as it was a matter of serious importance; he accordingly replied to me this evening, without – very properly – mentioning names, that The only way is to be quiet, and watch it.

Here ended this disgraceful subject, which makes one loath one's own sex; when they are bad, how disgracefully and disgustingly servile and low women are!! I don't wonder at men considering the sex despicable!

VICTORIA'S JOURNAL, 2 FEBRUARY 1839

ALICE ORR-EWING PLAYS
LADY FLORA HASTINGS

LADY FLORA HASTINGS

- LADY IN WAITING -

'This odious Flora business'
···· VICTORIA ····

ADY FLORA HASTINGS, who was born in 1806, was the daughter of a former Governor-General of India; her mother was a countess in her own right from an eminent Scottish family. She was tall, slim and graceful and people wondered why she had not married. No doubt it was the lack of a sufficient personal income, for she was 28 when she had first entered the Duchess of Kent's service in 1834 as a lady of the Bedchamber.

Flora was a gifted and intelligent woman; she was noted for her religious piety, but also had a sharp, if not cruel, wit and vivacity. At times she could seem rather aloof and was not always liked by those in the entourage. 'Lady Flora is civil to us all,' wrote one of the ladies of the Bedchamber, 'but restrained and uncommunicative: there will be no friendship with her.' Baroness Lehzen in particular suffered from her scathing remarks, for Hastings took delight in pandering to the Duchess's jealousy of Lehzen's increasing importance to her daughter.

Lady Flora was rewarded for her loyalty to the Duchess of Kent by promotion to lady in waiting; some thought she had now supplanted the daughter from whom the Duchess had become estranged. Others noted how often John Conroy was in Lady Flora's company – no doubt they were thrown together by their duties, but their close friendship was well known and the source of much gossip.

In the continuing battle with her mother after she came to the throne, Victoria became fixated on the idea that Lady Flora was spying on her – which in a way she may well have been – and reporting to Conroy on her every movement. She was therefore already primed to think badly of her. Once it was suggested to Victoria that Lady Flora had become pregnant by Conroy, her vivid imagination ran away with her.

WORD SOON REACHED LADY FLORA that a 'diabolical conspiracy' was brewing against her. She was convinced that Lehzen, whom she had always disliked, was the person stoking the fires. Victoria's own personal physician Sir James Clark was enlisted to make a medical examination, for it was the only thing that would satisfy the suspicions of the Queen and her ladies. In reality, Lady Flora had been feeling unwell and complaining of a pain in her side and 'bilious sickness' for some time. She had already consulted Sir James about it and he had offered a few simple but useless remedies for wind and constipation. She agreed to the examination, insisting that her own doctor also be present. But until then, she was informed, 'it was her Majesty's pleasure that I should not appear until my character was cleared by the means suggested'. Which indeed it was: the examination on 17 February showed that she was still a virgin. The cause of Lady Flora's distended belly was a tumour on the liver.

The Duchess of Kent was appalled: 'I cannot tell you how, and what I feel,' she told Lady Flora. 'The poor Queen has been led astray! It is shocking.' She responded by refusing to sit at her daughter's table until Lady Flora had been exonerated. A contrite Queen went to visit Lady Flora on 23 February and was shocked at what she saw:

> *She was dreadfully agitated and looked very ill, but on my embracing her, taking her by the hand, and expressing great concern and my wish that all should be forgotten – she expressed herself exceedingly grateful to me, and said, that for Mama's sake she would suppress every wounded feeling and would forget it.* ~VICTORIA'S JOURNAL, 23 FEBRUARY 1839

Although Lady Flora accepted the Queen's tearful apology she could not let her go without pointing out that 'I was treated as if guilty without a trial.' She was gracious enough also to accept apologies from other members of the court for maligning her, but only because the Duke of Wellington had advised her that it would injure the Queen if she held out any longer. Lady Flora described how Lady Portman came soon after 'to express her regret for having been most violent against me. I gave her my hand in token of forgiveness but when she asked to come to me afterwards I declined. It is one thing to forgive and another to forget. Thank God, I can do the first, but my memory is stubborn.'

B UT THAT WAS NOT THE END OF THINGS. To make matters worse for the inexperienced Victoria, the Lady Flora affair came hand in hand with a constitutional crisis. In May 1839, after a brief and happy initiation period with Lord Melbourne as her prime minister, he was forced out of office after only narrowly winning a vote in Parliament over the suspension of the Jamaican Constitution. His precarious majority was not sufficient to continue in government. Victoria, the self-possessed Queen, was reduced by this news to a petulant little girl:

> *All my happiness gone! That happy peaceful life destroyed, that dearest kind Lord Melbourne no more my minister [...] I took that kind, dear hand of his, and sobbed and grasped his hand in both mine and looked at him and sobbed out, 'You will not forsake me'; I held his hand for a little while, unable to leave go; and he gave me such a look of kindness, pity, and affection, and could hardly utter for tears, 'Oh! No,' in such a touching voice.*
>
> ~VICTORIA'S JOURNAL, 7 MAY 1839

VICTORIA:
I can't help it if my
friends are Whigs!

Having been brought up with Whig sympathies, Victoria did not take at all kindly to her beloved Lord Melbourne's place being taken by the stiff and formal Tory leader, Sir Robert Peel, whom she found 'such a cold, odd man'. Worse, a change in government also meant that some of her Whig ladies with links to Melbourne's ministry – notably her Mistress of the Robes, the Duchess of Sutherland, who was the sister of a prominent Whig – would also have to stand down, as a necessary gesture of confidence in Peel's new ministry. But Victoria baulked at what she considered interference in her personal affairs, and refused to contemplate the loss of her favourite ladies, several of whom were her closest allies in the continuing war with her mother. She was convinced that she would be surrounded by spies if they were replaced and wrote to Peel telling him that to remove them was 'repugnant to her feelings'. The forthright Peel's response to this stubborn refusal to cooperate, now known as the Bedchamber Crisis, was to declare himself unable to form a ministry. Victoria had in essence won and triumphantly she saw Lord M reinstated on 11 May – but it was a smear on her reputation that she had behaved so undemocratically.

Above: Sir Robert Peel –
'such a cold, odd man'.

VICTORIA MAY HAVE GOT WHAT she wanted when Melbourne was rapidly reinstated as prime minister, but in the intervening weeks the ominous shadow of the Lady Flora Hastings affair lingered. By late June, Lady Flora was dying a slow and agonising death and the court had been plunged into a sense of shame – 'full of bickerings and heart-burning' at her vicious persecution, according to diarist Charles Greville. On 27 June Victoria visited her in the Duchess's apartments, no doubt seeking a final message of forgiveness.

I went in alone; I found poor Lady Flora stretched on a couch looking as thin as anybody can be who is still alive; literally a skeleton, but the body very much swollen like a person who is with child; a searching look in her eyes, a look rather like a person who is dying; her voice like usual, and a good deal of strength in her hands; she was friendly, said she was very comfortable, and was very grateful for all I had done for her, and that she was glad to see me looking well. I said to her, I hoped to see her again when she was better, upon which she grasped my hand as if to say 'I shall not see you again'.

~VICTORIA'S JOURNAL, 27 JUNE 1839

On 5 July Lady Flora died, with the Duchess of Kent kneeling at her bedside. 'As her mother is not here, I wish to be in her place,' she had said. A post-mortem, conducted at Lady Flora's request, confirmed the enlargement of her liver and the cancer diagnosis. The whole disgraceful affair, which even Melbourne described as 'very awkward' for the Queen, was in fact deeply damaging. It had 'excited greater interest than any matter of a public and political character', observed Greville, and had 'played the devil with the Queen's popularity and cast dreadful odium and discredit on the Court'. The newspapers were full of it, with *The Times* taking the Queen's side and the *Morning Post*, which supported the Hastings family, launching a vicious attack. Scurrilous pamphlets were in circulation, too, with titles such as *The Palace Martyr* and *A Voice from the Grave of Lady Flora*. Baroness Lehzen was assumed to be part of the plot against poor, helpless Lady Flora and was derided as 'a low-born foreign woman of most

VICTORIA:
You don't understand how humiliating it is – to stand there and know that everyone is laughing at you.

MELBOURNE:
If I had stayed in my bedroom every time I saw something in the press I didn't like, I would still be there now.

forbidding aspect'. Lady Flora's brother was incensed, placing the ultimate blame at Melbourne's door for fuelling the gossip, and wanted to challenge him to a duel. The whole affair blew up to a full-scale scandal with the powerful and well-connected Hastings family demanding a public gesture of reparation from the Queen. Melbourne engaged in a frantic exercise in damage limitation on Victoria's behalf, writing conciliatory letters to Lady Flora's mother, assuring her that:

> *Her Majesty hastened to seize the first opportunity to testify to Lady Flora Hastings her conviction of the error of the impression which had prevailed, and her Majesty is still most desirous to do everything in her power to soothe the feelings of Lady Hastings and her family which must have been painfully affected by the events which have occurred.*
>
> ~LETTER FROM MELBOURNE TO
> THE MARCHIONESS OF HASTINGS, 12 MARCH 1839

It was too late. After Lady Flora's death, the Queen had to endure a period of intense unpopularity. She was openly booed at the theatre and hissed when she rode out in Hyde Park; at Ascot there were cries of 'Mrs Melbourne, where's your Lamb?' and both she and Melbourne were attacked in the press. The affair would mark one of the lowest points in the Queen's 63-year reign, and Victoria would be haunted ever after by her appalling error of judgement. It taught her the importance of never listening to or indulging in gossip and warned also, along with the Bedchamber Crisis, that no queen should act in such an inexcusably partisan way.

WHIGS vs TORIES

'*I always disliked the Tories, but now I quite hated them*'

···· VICTORIA ····

WHEN KING WILLIAM IV DIED in June 1837, a general election was called in which Sir Robert Peel's Tories were ranged against Lord Melbourne's Whigs. Both men had led their respective parties since 1834, Lord Melbourne representing Leominster and Peel representing Tamworth. In the election Melbourne won 344 seats to Peel's 314, a result which gave Melbourne a slim majority of 14 (330 being the minimum number of seats needed) and which showed that his party was in decline.

The Whigs and Tories had contested British politics since the 1680s, their rivalry based initially on religious difference. The Whigs had traditionally come from old, established aristocratic Protestant families, while the Tories had been supporters of the gentry and sympathetic to the Jacobite cause. By the time Victoria came to the throne the Whigs, who were essentially the precursors of the Liberal Party, were campaigning for parliamentary reform and for the greater accountability of the monarch to Parliament, while Sir Robert Peel's Tories were laying the foundations of the future Conservative Party.

Victoria had been brought up to be an ardent Whig supporter out of sentiment for her father, who had held strong Whig sympathies. In so doing, she stubbornly mistrusted the Tories in the most blinkered manner, even though it was clear by the end of William's reign that the Whigs as a political force were on the wane. Her passionate support for the old-school Whigs intensified with the arrival of her Whig prime minister, Melbourne contributing to her deeply undemocratic response to the Bedchamber Crisis of 1839. Ironically, her refusal to accept Melbourne's resignation and to remove her Whig ladies at Peel's request went directly against the reforming and democratic spirit of the Whigs, whom she claimed to so passionately support.

Said I always disliked the Tories, but now I quite hated them; and that I felt that I never could have any confidence in them, and that it would be against my nature.

~VICTORIA'S JOURNAL, 4 APRIL 1839

·······
Opposite: Robert Peel arriving at the House of Commons.

ALL IN ALL, 1839 HAD so far proved to be the most stressful and testing year for the young Queen; it had revealed a hard and priggish side to her nature and an unattractive strain of stubbornness and arrogance. 'Poor little Queen!' wrote the contemporary historian Thomas Carlyle:

> *She is at an age at which a girl can hardly be trusted to choose a bonnet for herself, yet a task is laid upon her from which an archangel might shrink.*
>
> ~THOMAS CARLYLE

So far, that task had been made bearable, as far as Victoria was concerned, by the presence of one man: her prime minister Lord Melbourne. 'The more I see of him and the more I know of him, the more I like and appreciate his fine and honest character […] and have always found him a kind and most excellent and very agreeable man. I am very fond of him.' By now Melbourne too – and much to his surprise – had found his tired and empty life entirely absorbed by his young Queen. For the stubborn and single-minded Victoria, nothing – not even the gossips – was going to keep her from her beloved prime minister.

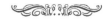

MELBOURNE:
Because we are so often together, we ride out most days, and I dine at the Palace nearly every night, it could be misconstrued.

LORD
M

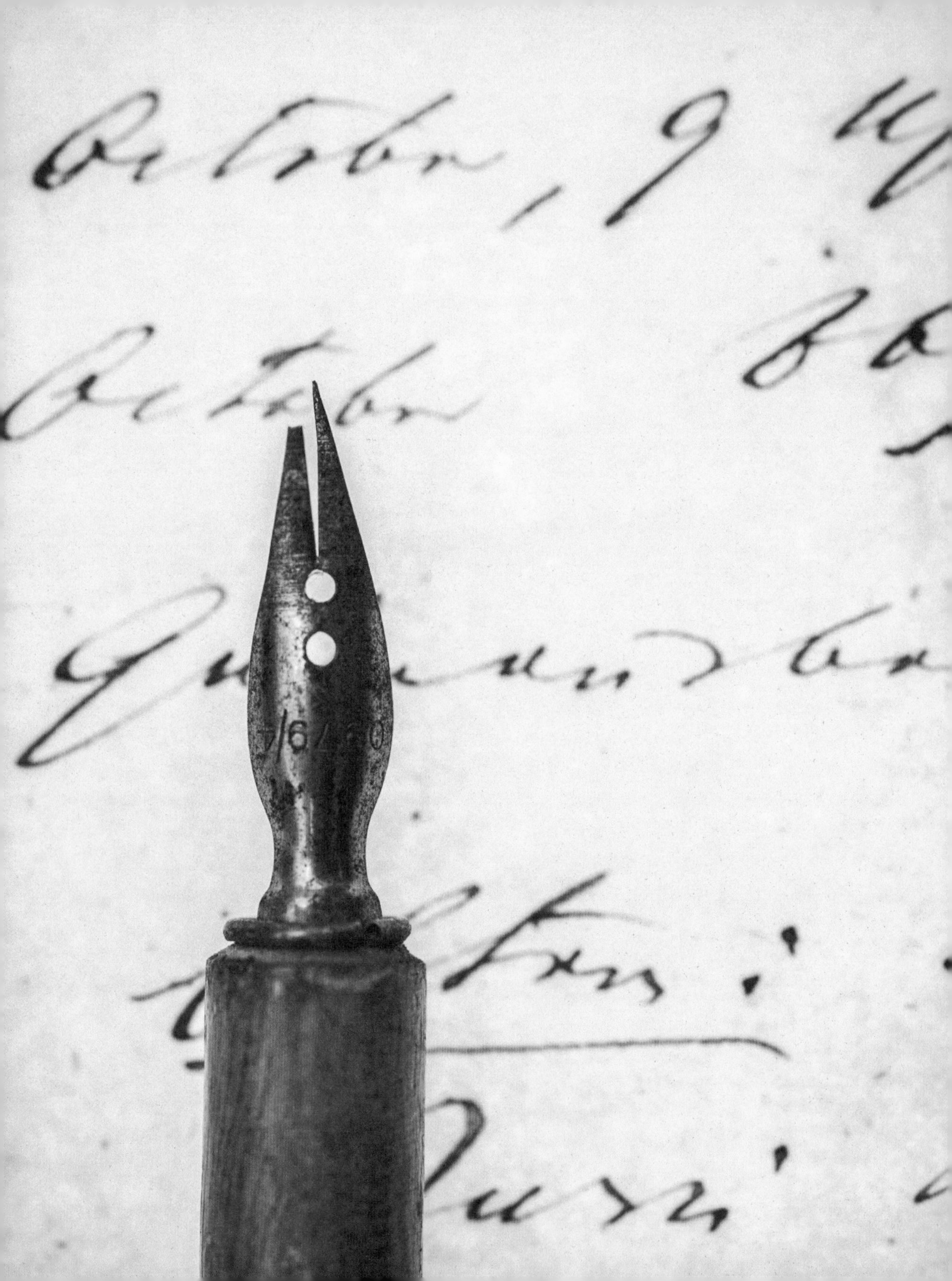

'I love this dear excellent man'

I
N THE HISTORY OF Queen Victoria's long reign, there were
several strong male figures who at various times exerted power
and influence over her, not least her beloved husband Albert. But
before her marriage, there is no doubt that a crucial, formative
influence came from perhaps the most unlikely of them all – her
first prime minister, William Lamb, 2nd Viscount Melbourne.

On the surface, this charming, handsome and worldly man who
preferred, if he could, to relax in his club and let life wash over him
would have seemed a rather jaded candidate for the important task
of moulding the mind of a young queen. In 1837, now aged 58, he had
been looking forward to retirement from political life. Instead, with
the accession of Victoria in June, he found himself entrusted with the
unique and challenging duty of instructing and developing 'the most
interesting mind and character in the world'. In this role he quickly
discovered that far more was expected of him than simple prime-
ministerial advice. Victoria also wanted to confide, to be entertained,
and to be kept company. Melbourne was her guru and wise counseller,
a surrogate father and arbiter of her tastes in the arts, the books she
read, the plays she saw. She soaked up his every word – on a wide range
of subjects – like blotting paper, and it would take all Melbourne's
considerable skill to maintain a distance, as romantic admirer, in order
to gently repel the intense ardour of her impressionable hero-worship.

THE TWO MEN MOST present in the young Victoria's life had been Sir John Conroy and Uncle Leopold. Sir John, of course, she despised and, once she was Queen, she quickly banished him from her household and from court. By 1839 he was effectively sent into exile, along with his wife and six children.

Leopold, on the other hand, was certainly a major influence. From the moment of his niece's birth, and as the self-appointed manager of the affairs of the House of Saxe-Coburg, Leopold had been mindful of the huge political advantage to be gained from seeing his niece safely on to the throne of Britain – a throne his dead wife Charlotte should have occupied.

From the mid-1830s, rejecting the overwhelming influence of Conroy and her mother, the young and guileless Victoria had grown increasingly dependent on the uncle she revered as a paragon of virtue. The long-winded homilies with which Uncle Leopold bombarded her ensured that she would look on him as a trusted adviser and father figure and she clung to his continuing presence, for she had no other strong male figure in whom she could confide. Uncle Leopold was perfection. He was, for Victoria, '*Il mio secondo padre* – or, rather, solo padre, for he is indeed like my real father, as I have none'.

Once she became Queen, however, and rapidly fell under the influence of her prime minister Lord Melbourne, there was a considerable shift in Victoria's relationship with Uncle Leopold. She began to resent his constant preaching on matters concerning British affairs of state and foreign policy. After a disagreement over British relations with Belgium in April 1839 she did not mince her words:

19th April 1839

I am glad I extracted some spark of politics from your dear Majesty, very kindly and nicely expressed. I know that your generous little heart would not have wished at any time but what was good for a country in which you were much beloved. But the fact is, that certainly your Government have taken the lead in maintaining a condition which time had rendered difficult to comply with ... We have not been listened to, and arrangements are forced on us ...

30th April 1839

My Dear Uncle,

I have to thank you for your last letters, which I received on Sunday. Though you seem not to dislike my political sparks, I think it is better not to increase them, as they might finally take fire, particularly as I see with regret that upon this one subject we cannot agree. I shall therefore limit myself to my expressions of very sincere wishes for the welfare and prosperity of Belgium ...

Victoria R

RUFUS SEWELL PLAYS LORD MELBOURNE

'He had a lovely way about him and was someone who really liked his fellow man. He was described as "the laziest prime minister in the history of Great Britain" because he had a great suspicion of anyone with a deeply fervent belief. He just liked the idea of making things work with people.'

LORD MELBOURNE

- VICTORIA'S FIRST PRIME MINISTER -

'*My excellent Lord Melbourne*'
···· VICTORIA ····

MELBOURNE WAS A CHILD of the Regency era, a former associate of the dandy Beau Brummell and a well-known ladies' man. Born into wealth and privilege, he was educated at Eton and Cambridge and entered Parliament almost by default in 1806. It was better than the Law, in which he had briefly and half-heartedly dabbled, but he admitted that its protracted and often mind-numbing debates were 'a dammed bore'. Having served briefly as prime minister in 1834, he had returned to the post in 1835.

But Melbourne was not a great believer in political reform or progress; all he really wanted to do was to drift pleasantly through life, enjoying the gossip of salon society at Holland House or lounge about with his feet on the sofa at his favourite clubs, Brooks's and The Reform. He certainly did not wish to have any demands placed upon him by such a young and inexperienced Queen. But in fact, in professional terms, he was very well equipped for the task. He was a Classical scholar, was extremely well read, had an encyclopaedic knowledge of political history and many years of experience in government behind him. Before long, he found himself slowly but surely seduced by the power of his unique position of influence over the Queen. How could he resist her natural vitality? Her childlike trust, her charm and curiosity all soon drew him in.

FOR THE FIRST THREE years of her reign, Victoria recorded every moment spent with Melbourne in the most effusive language – delighting in the fact that they often spent up to six hours a day together – and often quite alone. 'I esteem myself most fortunate to have such a man at the head of the Government; a man in whom I can safely place confidence,' she wrote within two weeks of coming to the throne. 'There are not many like him in this world of deceit!'

Her journal is filled with allusions to his likes and dislikes, down to his hatred of boiled mutton and rice pudding, and the pages echo to the constant repetition of 'Lord Melbourne said …' By January of 1838, such was their intimate friendship that she was referring to him simply as Lord M.

I love this dear excellent man who is kindness and forbearance itself, most dearly.

~VICTORIA'S JOURNAL, 23 SEPTEMBER 1839

....
Above: 'This dear excellent man' – Lord M instructing Victoria.

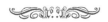

IN SUCH CONSTANT and close proximity, Melbourne's every comfort, thought and concern became the Queen's as well. She worried about his health, that the strains of a long day in Parliament left him pale, that he had enough sleep, that the Coronation ceremony might be too much for him, and she showered him with compliments and with gifts. In short, the Queen offered the ageing Melbourne the kind of affection that had been missing for so long in his life.

He in turn had a limitless supply of stories with which to entertain his young pupil during the many rather stultifying evenings that he spent with her at Buckingham Palace: 'There is no end to the amusing anecdotes and stories Lord Melbourne tells, and he tells them all in such an amusing funny way,' Victoria wrote with enthusiasm. There was nothing she relished more than his company after dinner, though Lord M greatly regretted not being allowed by her to dwell a little longer over the port with the gentlemen. Instead, he was obliged to look at picture albums, or listen to Victoria play the piano or sing. There were endless games of whist, charades or draughts too and he was even dragooned into playing shuttlecock. Here he was, 'evening after evening, talking with infinite politeness to a schoolgirl, bolt upright, amid the silence and the rigidity of Court etiquette' when in reality all he was longing for was home and bed. At times even the Queen couldn't help noticing how her prime minister's energy sagged until he would sometimes drop off in his chair and even snore.

But, as the diarist Charles Greville so perceptively observed:

He treats her with unbounded confidence and respect, he consults her tastes and her wishes, and he puts her at her ease by his frank and natural manners [...] He is so parental and anxious, but always so respectful and deferential [...] I have no doubt he is passionately fond of her as he might be of his daughter if he had one, and the more because he is a man with capacity for loving without having anything in the world to love.

~ CHARLES GREVILLE'S JOURNAL, 12 SEPTEMBER 1838

20 July 1839

The Queen anxiously hopes Lord Melbourne has slept well, and has not suffered from last night. It was very wrong of him not to wish the Queen good-night, as she expected he would in so small a party, for she saw that he did not go away immediately after supper. When did he get home? It was great pleasure to the Queen that he came last night.

LETTER FROM VICTORIA TO MELBOURNE, 20 JULY 1839

7 October 1839

The Queen sends the little charm which she hopes may keep Lord Melbourne from all evil, and which it will make her very happy if he will put it with his keys. If the ring is too small Lord Melbourne must send it back to her, and she will have it altered.

LETTER FROM VICTORIA TO MELBOURNE, 7 OCTOBER 1839

CRIMINAL CONVERSATION

MELBOURNE DID, HOWEVER, have something of a scandalous past, being accused of a 'criminal conversation' – an adulterous affair – on more than one occasion. *Crim con*, as it was commonly abbreviated to, was a legal term originating from the late eighteenth century, and usually involved a demand for compensation by a wronged husband from the adulterer. In polite conversation it came into general use as a euphemism for adultery in divorce cases.

In 1828 Lord Branden went to court for damages against Lord Melbourne for having an affair with his wife while Branden was serving as Chief Secretary for Ireland in Dublin. The case was dismissed. But he found himself accused of *crim con* again in the spring of 1836 when the Hon. George Norton brought an action against Melbourne for adultery with his wife. Melbourne had certainly for some time been friends with Mrs Norton and often stopped off at her home in Westminster on his way home from Whitehall or Parliament. But their association had never been more than an hour or so's conversation at a time, between friends. This case too was dismissed for lack of evidence, but for Melbourne as prime minister it was a very serious allegation and one that nearly resulted in the collapse of his government. He offered to resign but King William refused.

In court Melbourne's skilful counsel easily demolished the case against his client and after a nine-day trial the jury decided in his and Mrs Norton's favour. Melbourne came out of it with his reputation pretty much intact – enough, certainly, to continue as prime minister – but Caroline Norton's was ruined. She nevertheless remained a loyal friend of Melbourne's and courageously spent many years campaigning for the right of legally separated and divorced women to have custody of their children, having lost her own as a result of the 1836 court case. She also worked tirelessly for reform of the divorce laws. The use of the term 'criminal conversation' was abolished in 1857.

If Melbourne was something of a cynic, with a past history of being a roué, he also had a soft and sentimental side that responded to the Queen's youthful enthusiasm and ingenuousness. But he was a solitary and melancholy man. 'His mirth, though genial, came by fits and starts; the man was mournful in his heart of hearts,' as the poet Lord Lytton said of him.

Victoria sensed there was a sad side to him, for she knew that his marriage had ended unhappily. When he was 26 he had fallen in love with Lady Caroline Ponsonby, the daughter of the Earl of Bessborough, a pretty, quick-witted, red-haired woman with a reputation for being highly strung if not mentally unstable. The marriage had been happy at first, but the loss of a daughter at birth and the strain of caring for their epileptic and probably autistic son, Augustus, placed a great strain on the marriage.

Victoria had not wished to interrogate Melbourne further on the matter, but her natural curiosity was insatiable and eventually she got more of the story of Lord M and his wife Caro – as she was known – from the Duchess of Sutherland:

> *The Duchess of Sutherland spoke to me last night about Lady Caroline Lamb, Lord Melbourne's wife; she was [...] the strangest person that ever lived, really half crazy, and quite so when she died; she was not good looking, but very clever, and could be very amusing. She teased that excellent Lord Melbourne in every way, dreadfully and quite embittered his life [...] he was the kindest of husbands to her, and bore it most admirably; any other man would have separated from such a wife. He has now the greatest horror of any woman who is in any way eccentric or extravagant.*

> ~VICTORIA'S JOURNAL, I JANUARY 1838

At 2 I rode out with Lord Melbourne, dearest Lehzen, Miss Cavendish, Lord Fingall, Mr. Cooper, Col: Wemyss, and Col: Cavendish and c., and came home at a ¼ p.5. (...) I rode Comus who went beautifully; we rode very hard ~20 mile; to Swinley by Ascot Heath; we galloped up the course, and home by the Bagshot Road, and through Sheep Street (...) I rode the whole time between Lord Melbourne (whose horse went quiet, but was excessively eager, pulled and went a great pace) and Col: Cavendish. I was somewhat fearful lest this long and quick ride should tire my excellent Lord Melbourne. My beloved Daisy (Lehzen) bears these rides wonderfully, though I can't help feeling alarmed they should tire and exhaust her.

VICTORIA'S JOURNAL, 17 NOVEMBER 1838

HER MAJESTY'S
STIRRUP-HOLDER

'We galloped up the course'

···· VICTORIA ····

VICTORIA FIRST LEARNED to ride in 1832 when she was thirteen, and until her marriage in 1840 and the rapid arrival of her nine children, it was one of her favourite outdoor activities. She might have been small and round, standing at less than five foot tall, but on horseback in her velvet, Lincoln-green riding habit and top hat with veil draped round the brim, she immediately gained an innate majesty that many remarked on. Her teacher was James Fozard, based in the Royal Mews at Buckingham Palace, who was one of the best riding masters in London. He was given the official title of the Queen's Gentleman Rider and always accompanied her on rides.

Victoria showed great natural skill from the outset and was an extremely accomplished – if not daring – horsewoman, with boundless energy, who one observer noted seemed to be 'exhilarated with pleasure' when riding. She thought nothing of going for a 20-mile gallop around the Great Park at Windsor, or starting from Richmond Park out to Wimbledon Common and back via Vauxhall Bridge, accompanied by an entourage of 25 or 30 courtiers, with scarlet-coated outriders, riding ahead to clear their way. From Buckingham Palace she would ride out to Harrow, Willesden, Kilburn, the Edgware Road – in the days when these were all rural backwaters.

Baroness Lehzen found it all very taxing and a struggle to keep up. Lord Melbourne, too: despite being a good rider he came to dread the long, obligatory afternoon rides with the Queen. He was now in his late fifties and found such excursions exhausting.

After she came to the throne in 1837, Victoria was anxious to keep James Fozard on, but had difficulty thinking of a suitable royal appointment. In the end she created the new office of 'Stirrup-holder' especially for him. It is not clear exactly how long Fozard stayed in the post of 'Her Majesty's Stirrup-holder', but once she became pregnant with her first child in 1840 the excited accounts of breakneck horseback riding disappear from Victoria's journals.

....
Opposite, top left: Victoria – a natural and accomplished horsewoman.

IN 1812 THE HISTRIONIC CARO had gone off the rails, throwing herself into a torrid and very public six-month affair with the poet Lord Byron, who at that time was riding the tide of acclaim for his recent work *Childe Harold*. The humiliation for Melbourne, whose name was dragged through all the gossip columns, was terrible. Nevertheless, after the affair burnt itself out he took Caro back and cared for her till in 1825 he finally capitulated to her demand for a separation; she died three years later, her frail body worn down by heavy drinking and opiates.

Eventually, in April 1838, Melbourne told the Queen something of his feelings about Lord Byron, the man his besotted wife had summed up as 'mad, bad and dangerous to know':

> *He said he was extremely handsome; had dark hair, was very lame and limped very much; I asked if the expression of his countenance was agreeable; he said not; 'he had a sarcastic, sardonic expression; a contemptuous expression'. I asked if he was not agreeable; he said, 'He could be excessively so'; 'he had a pretty smile'; 'treacherous beyond conception; I believe he was fond of treachery'. Lord Melbourne added, 'he dazzled everybody', and deceived them; 'for he could tell his story very well'.*
>
> ~VICTORIA'S JOURNAL, 6 APRIL 1838

As for Melbourne's son, Augustus, he had tragically died in 1836. In her journal for 29 September 1837 Victoria recorded Melbourne's comment on the epilepsy that had afflicted his beloved son and the heartache this had caused him:

> *'It is a dreadful visitation and nothing can cure it; it destroys by degrees all the faculties of reason.' This he said in allusion to his poor son who died last year aged 29, and who was quite an idiot, caused by epilepsy; he was his only child and a very fine young man, they say. It is a dreadful thing. Lord Melbourne is so peculiarly kind-hearted, and feeling, a person who I think would be so happy to have a son, for he is so affectionate to his brother and sister and her children. As it was, they say he felt his poor boy's death very much, though it must have been a release.*
>
> ~VICTORIA'S JOURNAL, 29 SEPTEMBER 1837

3 October 1837

Lord Melbourne rode near me the whole time. The more I see of him and the more I know of him, the more I like and appreciate his fine and honest character. I have seen a great deal of him, every day, these last five weeks, and I have always found him in good humour, kind, good, and most agreeable. I have seen him in my Closet for Political Affairs, I have ridden out with him, (every day), I have sat near him constantly at, and after, dinner, and talked about all sorts of things, and have always found him a kind and most excellent and very agreeable man. I am very fond of him.

VICTORIA'S JOURNAL, 3 OCTOBER 1837

I F VICTORIA'S ATTACHMENT to her 'dear Lord M.' hadn't been overt to the court and her subjects, it became undeniable once Melbourne's majority in Parliament began to fail in May 1839. The news, she said, 'struck to my heart and I felt dreadfully anxious'. When later that morning he sent a letter confirming that he would have to resign, he urged her to 'meet this crisis with that firmness which belongs to your character, and with that rectitude and sincerity which will carry Your Majesty through all difficulties'.

But for once, his exemplary pupil failed him. She cried for days at the prospect of being deprived of her adored Lord M's daily company and her subsequent action was that of a stubborn, wilful girl and not a queen. Although Melbourne was persuaded to stay on, it was inevitable that such a close relationship between Queen and Prime Minister should provoke much gossip and innuendo. The 'Mrs Melbourne' tag, in circulation since the Flora Hastings affair, stuck:

> *She really has nothing to do with anybody but Melbourne, and with him she passes […] more hours than any two people, in any relations of life, perhaps, ever do pass together. This monopoly is certainly not judicious.*
>
> ~CHARLES GREVILLE'S JOURNAL, 15 DECEMBER 1838

Some of the newspapers were even suggesting that Victoria wished to marry Melbourne, adding to an increasing urgency in the minds of many at court and in government that the Queen should quash such rumours by finding a husband – and soon.

....
Right: Victoria's dear Lord M.

ALEX JENNINGS PLAYS LEOPOLD

LEOPOLD

'To hear dear uncle speak on any subject is like reading a highly instructive book'

···· VICTORIA ····

THE MOST INFLUENTIAL male presence in Victoria's early life was her uncle Leopold. Born in Coburg in 1790, he had been a dashing youth, with green eyes and fashionably combed-forward kiss-curls. The narcissist in him was careful to maintain this look in old age, along with lifts in his shoes to boost his height.

Leopold served in the Russian Imperial Army during the Napoleonic Wars, rising to the rank of General. In March 1814 as a member of Tsar Alexander I's entourage he was with the Russian army when it triumphantly entered Paris. It was Alexander who hatched the plan to see his protégé Leopold marry Charlotte, heir to the British throne, and in 1814 he took him to London.

As a member of the relatively small and lowly duchy of Saxe-Coburg-Saalfeld it was something of a coup for Leopold to land a Princess of Great Britain. He was seen as a clever interloper. At court and in London society Leopold was viewed as 'a Jesuit and a bore', 'a damned humbug'. Diarist Charles Greville didn't mince his words: Leopold was 'the shabbiest ass. His pomposity fatigues, and his avarice disgusts.' King William could not abide him either; he was a prissy teetotaller.

After his marriage to Charlotte ended prematurely in her tragic death in 1817, Leopold was consoled by a handsome annuity of £50,000, for life, from the British government. Ever a shrewd opportunist, he started looking for new openings. He travelled on the Continent, where he indulged his voracious sexual appetite in numerous affairs. He was living back in Coburg during 1818–19 when his nephew Prince Albert was born; rumours persist that Leopold was his real father.

Victoria's gratitude and admiration for Leopold were bottomless; even when he took the throne of Belgium in 1831 Leopold continued to offer pious pearls of wisdom from a distance. A year later he found himself another dynastic bride – Louise, daughter of Louis-Philippe, King of France, who was 22 years his junior. However, the hypocritical Leopold continued to have a string of mistresses.

·······

Opposite: Victoria's Uncle Leopold.

BY THE AUTUMN OF 1839 Uncle Leopold was exerting all his oily charm to try and bring to fruition the long-held project of his niece's marriage to his own preordained choice, her cousin, Albert of Saxe-Coburg. Victoria knew full well that if she should die before marrying and having children, her Uncle Cumberland, King of Hanover, would succeed to the British throne.

As an ultra-Tory, Ernest Augustus, Duke of Cumberland, was strongly opposed to a woman – his niece Victoria – becoming Queen. He was certainly furious that his brother the Duke of Kent, who had promised him he would not marry, had gone ahead and done so, and worse that the Duchess had given birth to a healthy child, thus thwarting his own designs on the British crown. Cumberland made no attempt to contain his deep jealousy of Victoria, and behind her back encouraged Sir John Conroy's claim that she was mentally unstable in his quest to secure a regency.

In 1837, when the Salic Law of Hanover prevented Victoria as a woman from taking the throne that was still jointly held by the British monarch, the Duke of Cumberland accepted it and removed himself to Hanover. But it was not until Victoria had her first child in November 1840 that he was no longer seen as a threat to her position as Queen.

Nevertheless, Victoria still had it in mind not to marry for another three or four years. In 1836, when Leopold had first raised the subject of Albert, she had conceded that he had seemed a perfectly agreeable candidate, but since then she had not given the matter much thought. That April she had told Melbourne emphatically '*my* feeling is quite against ever marrying', and she had been equally firm in reminding Uncle Leopold that she had made no commitment to Albert: 'There is no *engagement* between us,' she insisted.

But in October everything changed. After basking in the warm glow of a one-on-one political and social education with Lord M, Victoria's relationship with him experienced a dramatic sea change. It came with the arrival at Windsor of that young cousin from Saxe-Coburg. For whether she liked it or not, Albert's life, since their births only three months apart in 1819, had long since been inextricably bound up with hers.

PETER FIRTH PLAYS
THE DUKE OF CUMBERLAND

DUKE OF CUMBERLAND
- VICTORIA'S UNCLE -

'That old wretch'

Although Victoria had ensured the speedy dispatch of the overbearing Sir John Conroy after her accession to the throne, until she herself married and produced a living child to succeed her the heir apparent was her terrifying 'wicked uncle' Ernest Augustus, Duke of Cumberland. The bad-tempered, wolfish Duke with his sunken left eye and scarred, bewhiskered face (he was nicknamed Lord Wiskerandos after a character in a play by Sheridan) had been a lurking, sinister presence during the Queen's minority. He is often seen as the archetypal bogeyman, whom many at court suspected of wanting to wrest the throne from the young queen, but there is absolutely nothing to show that he ever wished Victoria any personal harm.

The Duke, who was born in 1771, grew up in Hanover and had a distinguished military career in the Hussars in the 1790s but became increasingly involved in politics after 1807. Any hopes of a political career were, however, wrecked when in 1810 he was involved in a scandal after his valet Joseph Sellis was found dead, with his throat cut. Ernest claimed the valet had attacked him – he certainly bore the head wounds to prove it – but although the official conclusion was that Sellis had killed himself, the press assumed that Ernest, with his reputation for brutality, had in fact murdered him.

It took some time for the Duke to be exonerated, the consensus being that the Corsican-born Sellis had attacked him for his virulently anti-Catholic sentiments. But the libellous rumours stuck. Further unsubstantiated claims that Cumberland had fathered his sister Sophia's illegitimate son also circulated, and the suggestion of an incestuous affair between them never went away.

THE GERMAN PAUPER

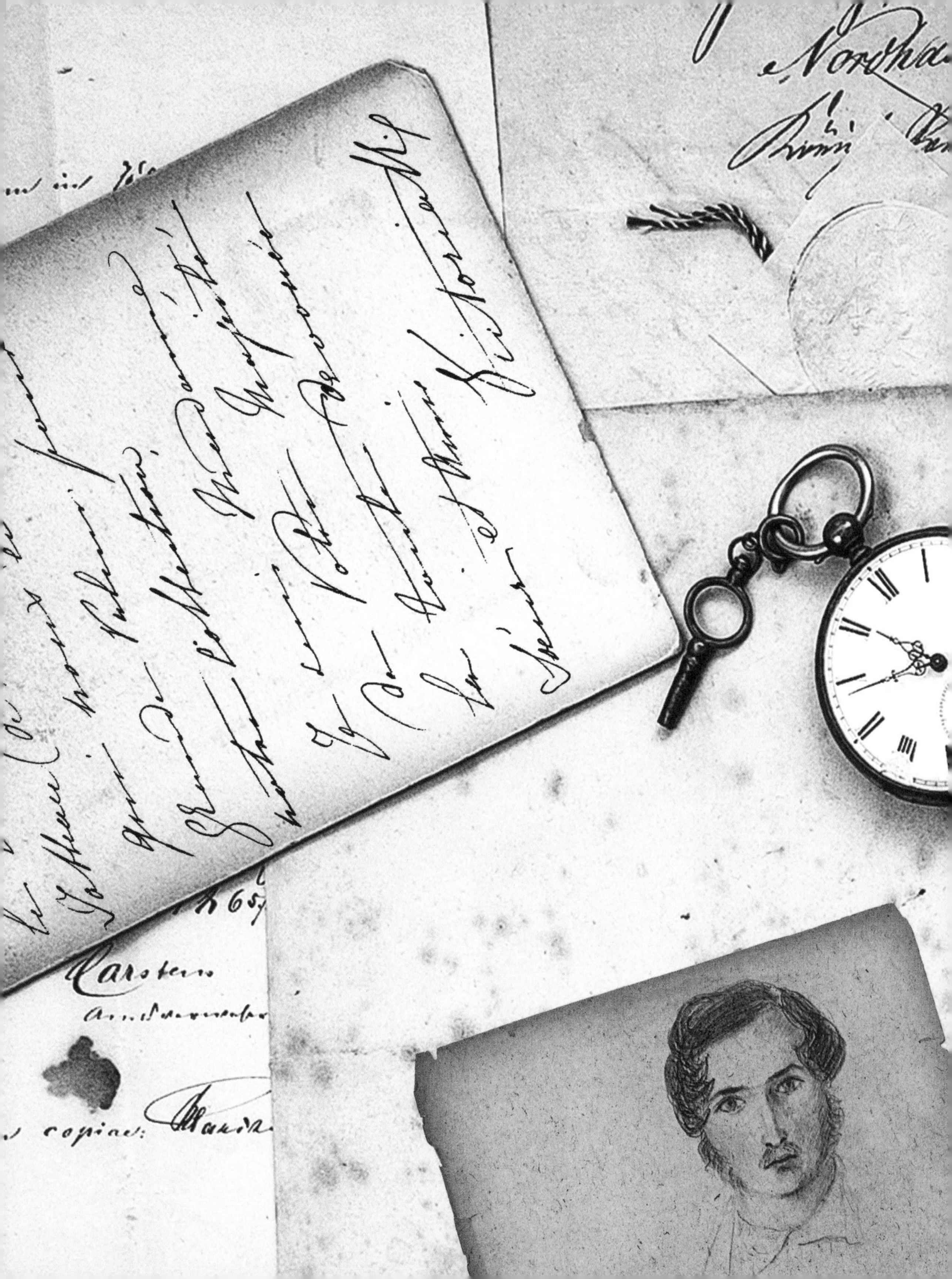

'It was with some emotion that I beheld Albert ... who is beautiful'

I N 1835 A VISITOR TO ASCOT was delighted to catch sight of the young Princess Victoria, in a large pink bonnet and rose-coloured satin frock 'which matched the roses on her cheeks' driving in the royal procession. He thought her 'quite unnecessarily pretty and interesting' but he felt sorry for her too:

> She will be sold, poor thing, bartered away by those great dealers in royal hearts, whose calculations will not be of much consolation to her if she happens to have a taste of her own.

But he was wrong; the heir to the throne would soon show that when it came to husbands she had very decided tastes of her own and would not be pushed into a marriage that she did not wish for.

·······
Right: Princess Victoria, aged 17: her satin dress 'matched the roses on her cheeks'.

A SUCCESSION OF ELIGIBLE candidates had been suggested for Victoria from as early as 1828, when she was approaching ten. Such premature discussion of Victoria's future shocked *The Times* newspaper, which dismissed any discussion 'of an infantine union or betrothment' and hoped that 'this matter will sink into oblivion for some eight or ten good years to come then'.

Alas it did not. Speculation revived in the mid-1830s, with the first and preferred choice of husband for Victoria being Prince George, son of Victoria's Uncle Cumberland. George was a logical choice, given that the thrones of Britain and Hanover were then tied, but he had lost his sight after an accident and although Victoria felt sorry for him, he was never a serious contender.

She showed no interest either in the next most obvious English candidate – her cousin Prince George of Cambridge. He too had the right credentials and had the Government's backing, and for a while the two mothers were hopeful of a match. But George did not like Victoria; he had an eye for prettier ladies. Dreading being pushed into a marriage against his will, he made a bolt for the Mediterranean, returning only after the Queen's engagement was announced. In November 1839, Victoria wrote to Melbourne 'to give him an account of the visit of the Cambridges'.

> *They were all very kind and civil, George grown but not embellished, and much less reserved with the Queen, and evidently happy to be clear of me.*
> ~LETTER FROM VICTORIA TO MELBOURNE, 18 NOVEMBER 1839

Over the years, the names of numerous foreign princes were bandied about as prospective husbands: the Duke of Orléans and the Duke of Nemours – both sons of the French King Louis-Philippe. The first found her far too short; the second was put off when he saw her demolish three bowls of soup in rapid succession at dinner. Still more were discounted: Charles, Duke of Brunswick was dismissed as an eccentric dandy, and an indifferent response from the Duchess of Kent to Prince Adalbert of Prussia sent him packing, for she favoured one of the Princes of Württemberg, who were her nephews.

CUMBERLAND:
You should go to the royal box now, George... Before she sits on that Russian's lap.

Ｆʀᴏᴍ ᴛʜᴇ ᴏᴜᴛsᴇᴛ King William had always had serious intentions about marrying his niece to one of the Princes of Orange (the sons of the Prince of Orange whom Princess Charlotte had dreaded having to marry). But Melbourne had raised numerous objections when he sounded him out about it and advised 'that in a political point of view, he did not think it a desirable thing; that the country would not like a connection with Holland'. William tended to agree, but the fact was that he was desperate to do anything to pre-empt a marriage for Victoria arranged by her mother – which almost certainly would mean to a German.

....
Above: Prince George of Cumberland, first
and preferred choice of husband for Victoria.

A SERIOUS ONSLAUGHT on the youthful Victoria's affections was launched in 1836 by her mother and uncle, who organised visits by a selection of suitable bridegrooms. The first to arrive, in March 1836, were Ferdinand and Augustus, the sons of Prince Ferdinand of Saxe-Coburg. Victoria found them 'both dear good young men' and seemed to take quite a shine to the tall and brown-eyed 20-year-old Ferdinand. At several balls arranged by her mother Victoria whirled round the dance floor in quadrilles with one or other brother and wept when Ferdinand left two weeks before his brother. It did not take her long to be consoled by Augustus. She was sixteen, a normal hormonal teenager, and her crushes came and went in waves like those of any schoolgirl.

Soon after, the Duchess of Kent and Uncle Leopold began plotting the visit of their nephews Ernest and Albert, sons of Duke Ernest of Saxe-Coburg-Gotha, a small Bavarian duchy no bigger than the county of Staffordshire. Five days from England by carriage and boat, it was known irreverently as 'The Stud Farm of Europe', and, by the end of the century, through Victoria's marriage to Albert, the Saxe-Coburgs would succeed in populating the royal houses of Great Britain, Belgium, Portugal and Bulgaria.

The King was furious when he heard the Duchess and Leopold were arranging this 'family visit' and declared that 'the Duke of Saxe-Coburg and his sons should never put foot in the country: they should not be allowed to land, and must go back whence they came'. Straight away he invited William and Alexander of Orange to England. When they arrived on 13 May and were introduced to Victoria at a ball at St James's Palace, she was not impressed and complained bitterly to Uncle Leopold of having had 'the dissatisfaction' of having them there:

The boys are both very plain and have a mixture of Kalmuck and Dutch in their faces, moreover they look heavy, dull and frightened and are not at all prepossessing. So much for the Oranges, dear uncle.

~LETTER FROM VICTORIA TO LEOPOLD, 17 MAY 1836

$\mathcal{S}$HE CHEERED UP, however, when, not long after the Oranges were dispatched, an exhausted Prince Albert, still suffering the bilious after-effects of terrible seasickness, arrived with his father and brother Ernest. Victoria was immediately impressed with the Saxe-Coburg brothers: they were charming and very musical and could draw well. The three of them passed a lot of time in each other's company, playing the piano, sketching, walking and riding in Kensington Gardens, and attending some functions in London. Writing to Uncle Leopold she said:

> *I must say that they are both very amiable, very kind and good, and extremely merry, just as young people should be; with all that, they are extremely sensible and very fond of occupation.*
>
> ~LETTER FROM VICTORIA TO LEOPOLD, 23 MAY 1836

But it was the gregarious Ernest with whom she was most taken; Albert, though 'so excessively handsome', seemed to have no stamina for staying up late and socialising.

Victoria was already perfectly well aware of course that Uncle Leopold had long since earmarked one or other of the two Coburg cousins for her. Although Duke Ernest had wanted his oldest son to marry Victoria, it was the younger brother Albert who had always been Leopold's choice. Victoria responded diplomatically by reminding her uncle that she was still only seventeen and far too young to marry, but she nevertheless thanked him 'for the prospect of great happiness you have contributed to give me, in the person of dear Albert'.

At this point, thankfully, Albert had passed muster; Victoria cooed all the appropriate and expected compliments about him in her journal, which she knew would be read by her mother, but as a candidate for her hand Albert was a prospect, nothing more. As Lord M later advised her, 'the Coburgs are not popular abroad and cousins are not very good things'.

....
Above top: 'So excessively handsome': Prince Albert, the Prince Consort.
Above: Ernest, the more gregarious of the two brothers.

DAVID OAKES PLAYS ERNEST

'Albert and Ernest were just over a year apart in age and they shared a room so they were best friends. They didn't have their mother around for most of their childhood and they were raised by a louche and excessively sexual father but they were everything to each other.

Albert was a bookworm, he loved the more mechanical side of life. Ernest was fun, the life and soul of the party and he's the one you'd want to hang out with.'

ERNEST
- ALBERT'S BROTHER -

'Honest and good-natured'
···· FEODORA ····

ALTHOUGH ERNEST HAD MANAGED to charm the young and impressionable Victoria on his visits in 1836 and 1839, he was rather ugly and not very bright, so much so that he was nicknamed 'The Clown of Coburg'. He was liked by many, however, including Victoria's sister Feodora. Writing to Victoria in 1836, she said, 'Ernest is my favourite, although Albert is much handsomer and cleverer, but Ernest is so honest and good-natured.'

Like many of those seduced by Ernest's superficial charms, Feodora was utterly oblivious to the dark and unpleasant character that lurked beneath. For in reality he was a serial sex pest like his father, spending much of his income on prostitutes and brothels. Wherever he went in Europe he considered women fair game, and married diplomats were warned to leave their wives and daughters at home.

Ernest and Albert's father had by this point married his niece, by whom he had no children, although in 1838 he had twins by a servant girl. In the end he paid the price of his compulsive libidinous behaviour by contracting syphilis. History repeated itself in the case of Ernest. When he arrived in England for Victoria and Albert's wedding in 1840, he fell ill with venereal disease and was undergoing treatment for it at the very time Victoria was making flattering comments about him in her journal.

Albert, of course, was well aware of his brother's problem and wrote a very strong letter to him: 'I must advise you as a loving brother to give up all ideas of marriage for the next two years and to work earnestly for the restoration and consolidation of your health…to marry would be as immoral as dangerous…for you. If the worst should happen, you would deprive your wife of her health and honour, and should you have a family, you would give your children a life full of suffering…and your country a sick heir. At best your wife could not respect you and her love would thus not have any value for you.'

Two years later Ernest married Princess Alexandrine of Baden and infected her with syphilis.

WHEN VICTORIA CAME to the throne in June 1837 she found herself engulfed by an outburst of 'Reginamania' that was sweeping Britain. It was not just princes and their parents who thought themselves eligible for the Queen's hand: a mass of letters, declaring passionate love and proposals of marriage, began pouring in to Buckingham Palace from a succession of stalkers and admirers, all insisting they would make the perfect Consort. Some of those admirers – who were dubbed 'The Queen's Lovers' in the press – even succeeded in infiltrating the grounds of Buckingham Palace.

Insatiable curiosity about Victoria had been filling the papers at a time when the Victorian press was beginning to exploit its access to a mass reading public, and they went to town on every detail. One of the first, a man named Captain John Goode, whom the press described as 'labouring under the delusion that he was one day destined to possess Her Majesty's hand', had begun stalking Victoria when she was still a princess and living at Kensington Palace. He had even tailed her on holiday to Ramsgate and Hastings. On numerous occasions he was found hanging around outside Kensington Palace 'inquiring at the grand entrance the state of the Queen's health, and endeavouring to get in, for the purpose of writing his name in the visiting book'.

Despite being escorted out of Kensington Gardens he repeatedly made his way back in, in the hope of catching sight of Victoria. When her carriage emerged through the gates to take her on a drive, he would follow in his own phaeton. If they stopped and got out he would jump out and try to accost her. Goode, it appeared, was convinced he was the son of George IV and the rightful heir to the throne. On one occasion he sprang up at the side of the Queen's carriage and shouted, 'I'll have you off your throne, and your mother too.' He was arrested several times for harassing the Queen and in November 1837 was committed to the Bethlem lunatic asylum.

ELSEWHERE, AN ARDENT admirer got into the Chapel
Royal in order to declare his love for the Queen; another,
a captain in the Light Dragoons called Tom Flower, tried to infiltrate
the Coronation ceremony at Westminster, having failed to get
into the Queen's box at the opera, and was hauled off to Tothill
Fields House of Correction.

Several tried to stop the Queen's horse when she was out riding;
a Ned Hayward did so in Hyde Park in order to hand her a letter
asking if she would marry him. John Stockledge, who was celebrated
by the satirical press as 'The Queen's Last Lunatic Lover', also made
a nuisance of himself in the winter of 1837. A wholesale tea merchant
from Manchester, he had spent time in lunatic asylums in Liverpool
and Lancaster and claimed to be the rightful King of England.

On 29 November he arrived at Windsor Castle (which at that
time had no sentries) and on seeing a porter on duty at the lodge said,
'I demand entrance into the castle as King of England', to which the
porter replied, 'Very well, Your Majesty, but be pleased to wait until
I get my hat.' He then took Stockledge into the castle and handed
him over to the police. When questioned about his attempt to gain
entry, Stockledge had said that 'he was like all other men who
wanted wives – he was looking after one'.

AFTER ALBERT'S RETURN to Saxe-Coburg
he and Victoria exchanged occasional letters.
Although she accepted the probability of marriage
to him she continued to insist that they were both
too young and inexperienced and Albert's English
was simply not good enough. From a distance,
therefore, she took an interest in Albert's grooming
for the role, which was undertaken by Leopold's
close friend and adviser Baron Stockmar, who
arranged Albert's education, first with tutors in
Brussels and then at Bonn University – all with
the intention of creating in him the perfect
Prince Consort.

....
Right: Windsor Castle.

By 1839 Stockmar thought Albert was ready; he reported to Leopold that his protégé was endowed with all the right qualities 'likely to please the sex and that his mental qualities were also of a high order'. But Victoria at this point had dug in her heels and was still talking of another three or four years before marrying. On 15 July she told Uncle Leopold:

> *Though all the reports of Albert are most favourable, and though I have little doubt I shall like him, still one can never answer beforehand for feelings, and I may not have the feeling for him which is requisite to ensure happiness. I may like him as a friend, and as a cousin, and as a brother, but no more.*
>
> ~LETTER FROM VICTORIA TO LEOPOLD, 15 JULY 1839

While Leopold and Victoria were discussing Albert's finer points as though he were a stallion at stud, Albert himself became annoyed and impatient. His pride was wounded and he threatened to withdraw. He was persuaded to visit Victoria again with Ernest in October, by which time word had got back to Victoria about his reluctance. She was not amused: 'I think they don't exhibit much *empressement* [urgency] to come here, which rather shocks me.' Meanwhile, she had that May been enchanted by a visit from the heir to the Russian throne, Grand Duke Alexander Nikolaevich, who had flattered her and whispered sweet nothings in French in her ear, and propelled her round the dance floor till three in the morning, as she recounted in a letter to Melbourne:

> *The Queen danced the first and the last dance with the Grand Duke, made him sit near her, and tried to be very civil to him, and I think we are great friends already and get on very well; I like him exceedingly.*
>
> ~LETTER FROM VICTORIA TO MELBOURNE, 11 MAY 1839

He was so strong, so handsome in his Hussar's uniform, and she thought she might just be in love …

ENTERTAINING A GRAND DUKE OF RUSSIA

– THE VISIT OF THE TSAREVICH, ALEXANDER NIKOLAEVICH IN MAY 1839 –

VICTORIA'S FIRST EXPERIENCE of entertaining foreign royalty came in May 1839 when the heir to the Russian throne, Grand Duke Alexander Nikolaevich, arrived in London on an unofficial visit.

It was the first visit of a Russian VIP since Alexander I had come to England in 1814 as an ally during the Napoleonic Wars. Victoria had little warning of the visit and admitted to Lord M that she was 'quite cross about it'. She changed her tune somewhat when Alexander arrived, for he was 'tall with a fine figure, a pleasing open countenance without being handsome, fine blue eyes, a short nose and a pretty mouth with a sweet smile'. Alexander brought with him a trunkful of diamond inlaid boxes and enormous diamond rings, which he proceeded to distribute to the great and the good. For the sake of propriety, he was mostly accommodated not by the Queen, but at Mivart's Hotel (now Claridge's). When Victoria invited him to spend three days at Windsor there was considerable disapproval.

During Alexander's stay he was wined and dined by the British aristocracy. He visited Ascot, Woolwich Barracks, Oxford and even the Tothill Fields of Correction in London, where he asked for a list of all those imprisoned for debts under £5 and cleared them all. Victoria invited him to the Italian opera – though protocol dictated they should sit in separate boxes. Tongues were set wagging, however, when during the interval Alexander slipped into Victoria's box for a chat – behind a drawn curtain. Members of the Russian entourage noticed a fair degree of flirting between them and a dispatch was sent to Tsar Nicholas in Russia:

> *The Queen is clearly enjoying the society of His Imperial Majesty. Everyone is saying they are an ideal couple. Were the Grand Duke to make a proposal to the Queen, it would be accepted without hesitation.*
>
> ~DISPATCH TO TSAR NICHOLAS, MAY 1839

There was, of course, no possibility of Victoria marrying a Russian grand duke, but it greatly alarmed the Tsar, who knew how impetuous his son was. He did not want Alexander to even contemplate playing second fiddle to the English queen – any more than Victoria would have wanted to share power with a Russian. Tsar Nicholas immediately ordered Alexander to Darmstadt, where soon after he became engaged to Princess Marie of Hesse.

At the end of his visit Alexander enjoyed a dinner in the magnificent St George's Hall in the State Apartments at Windsor. It 'looked beautiful', the Queen noted:

At a little after 12 we went into the dining-room for supper; after supper they danced a Mazurka for ½ an hour, I should think nearly; the Grand-Duke asked me to take a turn, which I did [...] the Grand-Duke is so very strong, that in running round, you must follow quickly, and after that you are whisked round like in a Valse, which is very pleasant [...] I never enjoyed myself more. We were all so merry; I got to bed by a ¼ to 3, but could not sleep till 5.

~VICTORIA'S JOURNAL, 27 MAY 1839

On leaving England, having handed out £20,000 to various charities and the needy, Alexander made one parting gift. He donated £300 to the Jockey Club. In gratitude, the club established a race in his honour – the Cesarewitch Handicap, which has been run at Newmarket ever since. As he said farewell to Victoria on 29 May, he told her how touched he was by the reception he had received in England:

[He] trusted that all this would only tend to strengthen the ties of friendship between England and Russia [...] I kissed his cheek; upon which he kissed mine (cheek) in a very warm affectionate manner and we again warmly shook hands. [...] I felt so sad to take leave of this dear amiable young man, whom I really think (talking jokingly) I was a little in love with.

~VICTORIA'S JOURNAL, 29 MAY 1839

The handsome Alexander was gone, but Victoria consoled herself by playing the Grand Duke's favourite quadrille – 'Le Gay Loisir'.

....
Right: Alexander II of Russia: 'I kissed his cheek'.

BUT WHEN ALBERT ARRIVED in October, all others were forgotten. After a three-and-a-half-year gap, Victoria experienced a magical moment that has since been immortalised. Setting eyes on Prince Albert again, she was stunned to see that the the gawky German frog had morphed into an archetypal Prince Charming:

> *At ½ p. 7 I went to the top of the staircase and received my 2 dear cousins Ernest and Albert – whom I found grown and changed, and embellished. It was with some emotion that I beheld Albert.*
> ~VICTORIA'S JOURNAL, 10 OCTOBER 1839

PENGE:
What do you think, Mrs Jenkins? Is Her Majesty partial to a little Coburg sausage or not?

Thereafter, she gushed in her journal about Albert's charm and how 'excessively handsome' he was. He had 'such beautiful blue eyes, an exquisite nose, and such a pretty mouth with delicate moustachios and slight but very slight whiskers; a beautiful figure, broad in the shoulders and a fine waist'. To top it all, he was a wonderful dancer. On 11 October when they danced together she gave him a flower from her bouquet. Having no buttonhole in which to fix it, Albert took out a small penknife and, cutting a slit in his uniform, placed the flower over his heart. It was enough to make any romantically minded 20-year-old girl swoon; Victoria wasted no time in making up her mind to marry and in securing Lord M's approval. He was delighted: 'I think it is a very good thing, and you'll be much more comfortable; for a woman cannot stand alone for long, in whatever position she is,' he told her.

Above: Prince Albert: 'such beautiful eyes'.

My Dearest Uncle,

Uncle Ernest and my cousins arrived here on Wednesday, sains et saufs. Uncle is looking remarkably well, and my cousins are most delightful young people. I will give you no detailed description of them, as you will so soon see them yourself. But I must say, that they are both very amiable, very kind and good, and extremely merry, just as young people should be; with all that, they are extremely sensible, and very fond of occupation. Albert is extremely handsome, which Ernest certainly is not, but he has a most good-natured, honest, and intelligent countenance. We took them to the Opera on Friday, to see the Puritani, and as they are excessively fond of music, like me, they were in perfect ecstasies, having never heard any of the singers before . . .

LETTER FROM VICTORIA TO LEOPOLD, 23 MAY 1836

My Dearest Uncle,

These few lines will be given to you by my dear Uncle Ernest when he sees you. I must thank you, my beloved Uncle, for the prospect of great happiness you have contributed to give me, in the person of dear Albert. Allow me, then, my dearest Uncle, to tell you how delighted I am with him, and how much I like him in every way. He possesses every quality that could be considered to render me perfectly happy. He is so sensible, so kind, and so good, and so amiable too. He has, besides, the pleasing and delightful exterior and appearance you can possibly see. I have only now to beg you, my dearest Uncle, to take care of the health of one, now so dear to me, and to take him under your special protection. I hope and trust that all will go on prosperously and well on this subject of so much importance to me. Believe me always, my dearest Uncle, your most affectionate, devoted and grateful Niece

LETTER FROM VICTORIA TO LEOPOLD, 7 JUNE 1836

TOM HUGHES PLAYS ALBERT

'Victoria was very young when she came to the throne, and Albert, like Melbourne, was someone she could trust in a world of sycophants, trying to gain her favour for their own benefit. With Albert there's an emotional strength and an integrity that was probably challenging to Victoria but quite attractive. Although he had to be subservient to a certain degree, because of etiquette, there was an equality to their relationship. No one wants a puppy dog.'

ALBERT

'He is so sensible, so kind, and so good'

···· VICTORIA ····

Prince Albert of Saxe-Coburg-Gotha was the son of Duke Ernest I and Louise of Saxa-Gotha Altenburg. His parents had married in 1816, an expedient dynastic arrangement on the part of his father in which the pretty and intelligent Louise suffered and her private fortune was rapidly spent. Ernest had endless extramarital affairs and fathered three illegitimate children. Out of revenge and loneliness Louise began to take lovers too. A son, also called Ernest, was born to the couple in 1818 and in May 1819 a second son, Albert. But the Duke soon tired of Louise and in August 1824 he expelled her from Coburg; she never saw her two sons again. In 1826 Louise remarried but died of cancer of the womb in 1831. Even though he saw nothing of her after the age of five, Prince Albert would always be haunted by her loss.

Prince Albert spent most of his young life at Rosenau, the Gothic-style hunting lodge four miles from Coburg, where he developed a very deep bond with the surrounding Thuringian forest. As he grew older, he changed from a shy and rather pudgy young man into a very handsome, well-read and accomplished prince. Albert's studies at university, and his training in fencing, riding and dancing, were followed by an educational tour of southern Germany, Switzerland and Italy to admire the art. He came out of it with a good education, exceptionally good taste in art and music, and – miraculously for the times – with a still spotless reputation.

I have caused you to be assembled at the present time, in order that I may acquaint you with my resolution in a matter which deeply concerns the welfare of my people, and the happiness of my future life.

It is my intention to ally myself with the (sic) Prince Albert of Saxe-Coburg and Gotha. Deeply impressed with the solemnity of the engagement which I am about to contract, I have not come to this decision without a mature consideration, nor without feelings of strong assurance that, with the blessing of Almighty God, it will at once secure my domestic felicity, and serve the interests of my country.

I have thought fit to make this resolution known to you at the earliest period, in order that you may be fully apprised of a matter so highly important to me, and to my kingdom, and which I persuade myself will be most acceptable to all my loving subjects.

Victoria R

VICTORIA'S STATEMENT ON HER MARRIAGE TO
THE PRIVY COUNCIL, 23 NOVEMBER 1839

O N 15 OCTOBER 1839, with confidence in her unique royal prerogative, which meant that she had to propose to *him*, Victoria asked Albert to come to her little Blue Closet Room.

At about half past 12, I sent for Albert. He came to the Closet where I was alone, and after a few minutes I said to him, that I thought he must be aware why I wished them to come here, and that it would make me too happy if he would consent to what I wished (to marry me).

We embraced each other over and over again, and he was so kind, so affectionate; oh! to feel I was, and am, loved by such an Angel as Albert, was too great delight to describe! he is perfection; perfection in every way, in beauty, in everything!

~VICTORIA'S JOURNAL, 15 OCTOBER 1839

LEOPOLD:
Normally it is the man who must declare his love, but in your case you will have to overcome your maidenly modesty and propose to Albert.

All thought of postponing her marriage for another three or four years vanished: 'Seeing Albert has changed all this.' Albert was overwhelmed and wrote to his stepmother in Coburg, telling her, 'The joyous openness of manner in which she told me this quite enchanted me. And I was quite carried away by it.' He was 'puzzled to believe that I should be the object of so much affection'. For Victoria's love, once the floodgates were opened, was, as he was beginning to discover, a never-ending torrent.

It is said that after Albert returned to Coburg the Queen missed him so dreadfully that she spent her time singing 'only German songs', many of which they had sung together during his visit. In sympathy, romantically minded young women up and down the land were soon warbling a popular German ditty translated as 'I Caught Her Tear at Parting'. It was sold for two shillings as 'Prince Albert's Parting Song' and became the Victorian equivalent of a chart topper.

....
Right: 'He is perfection': Albert courting Victoria.

After Albert returned to Coburg to prepare for the wedding, there was a striking new air of resolution in the young Queen's manner. Prince Albert was to be invested with the Order of the Garter and given the rank of Field Marshal in the British Army; he would also be naturalised as a British citizen and be thereafter titled His Royal Highness. But even the malleable Lord M baulked at Victoria's demand that he be made 'King Consort': 'For God's sake, let's hear no more of it, Ma'am,' he said, 'for if you once get the English people into the way of making kings, you will get them into the way of unmaking them.'

Victoria also tried securing a handsome income from Parliament for her future husband. In January Lord John Russell proposed an allowance of £50,000, the amount that Prince Leopold – 'that unwelcome foreigner' – had received. Public resentment to another German pauper prince, particularly from the House of Saxe-Coburg, marrying into the royal family was considerable. Popular ballads such as 'The German Bridegroom' derided Albert as a fortune hunter.

It was a time of considerable economic difficulty in Britain and the Queen had not yet won back the affection of her people after the debacle of the Bedchamber Crisis and the Lady Flora Hastings affair. In Parliament, the radical MP Joseph Hume argued that 'to set a young man down in London with so much money in his pocket was a most dangerous thing to do'. The Commons roared with laughter at this and a Tory amendment reduced the allowance to £30,000.

> At near 11 Lord M. received a note from Stanley saying that we had been beat by 104; that it had been made quite a party question (vile, confounded, infernal Tories), that Peel had spoken and voted against the £50,000 (nasty wretch), and Graham too. As long as I live, I'll never forgive these infernal scoundrels, with Peel at their head, as long as I live for this act of personal spite!! ~VICTORIA'S JOURNAL, 27 JANUARY 1840

Much to Victoria's annoyance, Parliament refused to pass a Precedency Clause giving the Prince the same royal status as his wife and also turned down her request for him to be given a peerage.

He comes the bridegroom of Victoria's choice,
The nominee of Lehzen's vulgar voice;
He comes to take, 'for better or for worse',
England's fat queen and England's fatter purse.
– The German Bridegroom

THE GERMAN PAUPER

FOR THE HIGHLY SENSITIVE ALBERT, receiving a reduced allowance was a slap in the face; he told Uncle Leopold that he was 'shocked and exasperated by the disrespect' shown him. Even from a distance, he had become painfully aware of the hostile reception that awaited him in a country already disposed not to like him as both a German and a foreigner. The satirical press was already lampooning him for his German accent and his stiff and starchy Teutonic manner. He therefore contemplated his future with mixed emotions. Dreading having to leave behind his intimate and sheltered world in Coburg, he wrote with some apprehension about what lay ahead:

> With the exception of my relations toward [the Queen] my future will have its dark sides, and the sky will not always be blue and unclouded. But life has its thorns in every position, and the consciousness of having used one's powers and endeavours for an object so great as that of having promoted the good of so many, will surely be sufficient to support me.
> ~LETTER FROM ALBERT TO HIS STEP-MOTHER, 5 NOVEMBER 1839

Marriage to Victoria, from Albert's point of view, was not just a matter of love but of duty, a mission to be useful, and it involved a degree of sacrifice. But for Victoria, love was absolutely everything.

> Setting aside that he is my brother, I esteem and love him more than any man on earth. You will smile, perhaps, if I speak to you of him in such high terms of eulogy! But I do it in order that you may feel still more what you have gained in him! As yet, you are most taken with his manner, so youthfully innocent, his tranquillity, his clear mind – this is as he appears at first acquaintance. Knowledge of men & experience – one would read less in his face; and why? Because he is pure before the world and before his own conscience; not as if he did not yet know sin, the earthly temptations, the weakness of men no, but because he knew and still knows how to struggle with them, supported by the incomparable superiority & firmness of his character.
> ~LETTER FROM ERNEST TO VICTORIA, 19 DECEMBER 1839

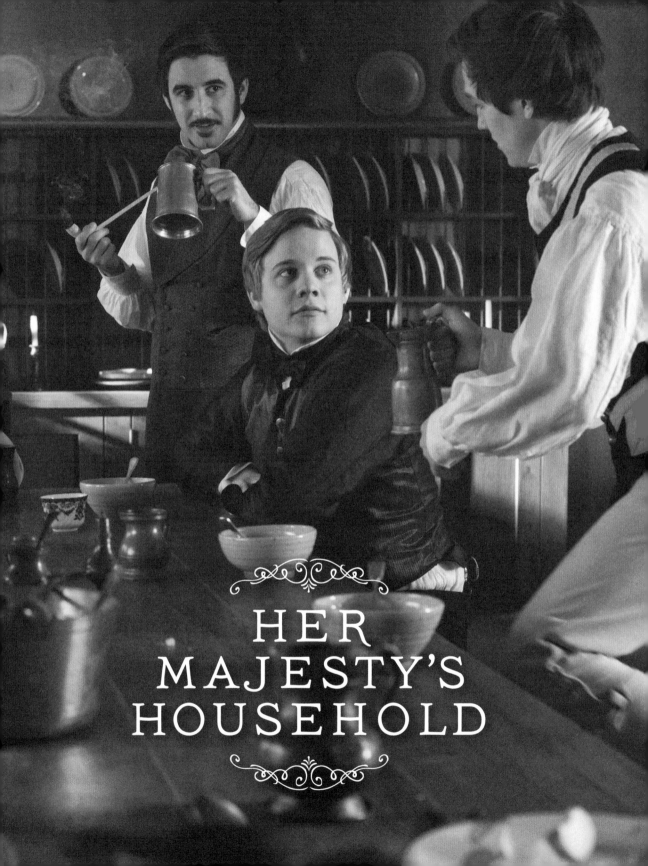

HER MAJESTY'S HOUSEHOLD

'keep people in their place and at a proper distance'

···· VICTORIA ····

BEHIND THE SCENES at her homes at Buckingham Palace and Windsor Castle, Queen Victoria's daily life and comforts were served by a huge retinue of servants, the vast majority of whom she never saw or came into any contact with. While protocol and etiquette ruled among the lords and ladies in the court above stairs, a similar rigid pecking order prevailed among the largely faceless and nameless servants below. Victoria had numerous and lengthy conversations with Lord M soon after her accession about how she intended to manage them.

> *Spoke of the Maids of Honour's and Bedchamber Women's salaries; about the Lords', Grooms', Equerries', and Clerk Marshall's salaries; I spoke to him about many things concerning the gentlemen, Maids of Honour, &c.; said it was necessary to keep people in their place and at a proper distance; Lord Melbourne observed with great truth and right feeling upon all this, and said it was absolutely necessary to be able to tell people often what they did not like; said if this was done at the beginning they would not try again to do what they should not; he added (in consequence of my saying that it was necessary to keep the Maids of Honour at a right distance, and which was perhaps more difficult on account of my great youth), 'they begin by being familiar, and which always ends in an attempt to govern'. He spoke most sensibly and reasonably about all this.*
>
> ~VICTORIA'S JOURNAL, 30 JANUARY 1838

AN ACT OF PARLIAMENT on 23 December 1837 set the allowance for running the Queen's Household at £385,000 per annum – around £41 million today. However, the system the Queen inherited when she moved into Buckingham Palace that year was far from efficient. In fact, it was downright antiquated and plagued with malpractice and political partisanship. The various and clearly defined functions of a total household of some 445 people were overseen by three different officials, all of them aristocrats, who ran three entirely separate departments, and whose appointments were dictated by change of government.

The Lord Chamberlain was the most senior member of the Household; his post was always given to a nobleman by the government in power. He dealt with all the domestic staff who worked above stairs and who served or officiated at court ceremonies and official functions and with the tradesmen who maintained the interior of the palaces. The Lord Steward was in charge of the hundreds of domestic servants who worked below stairs in the kitchens, pantries, sculleries, storerooms and laundries of the palace. The Master of the Horse ensured the upkeep of the Queen's carriages, instructed their drivers and organised the stabling and care of her horses; the royal equerries also came under his jurisdiction. The maintenance of the fabric of the royal palaces and their grounds was the province of yet another department – the Office of Woods and Forests.

There were, in addition, a wide range of personal appointments made by the Queen for professional services which further added to the huge running costs of her Household: the physicians, surgeons and apothecaries – extraordinary and in-ordinary – as well as sculptors, painters, chaplains, photographers, musicians, dentists, and even a resident rat killer and chimney sweep. In addition, and for the first time, a new appointment was created, that of the Queen's permanent hairdresser. A Monsieur Isidore Marchand was selected at a salary of £400 p.a. His salary and that of the Queen's two dressers and two wardrobe maids – amounting to £880 per year – were paid by Victoria from the personal allowance for her toilette of £6,000 p.a.

THE COMPLEX DIVISION of roles within the Royal Household, under different supervisors, inevitably created endless and frustrating anomalies; there was often insufficient supervision of staff above and below stairs; guests lost their way in the badly lit corridors of Buckingham Palace where no one was on duty to help them; and many of the servants, of whom there were too many, simply did not have enough to do. Boredom often prevailed. There is no doubt that food was frequently purloined from the royal pantries, and candles in every room were changed daily and unnecessarily. One of the well-known perks enjoyed by servants, as the TV series illustrates, was the trade in candles. A wax-chandler's shop in Piccadilly, opposite St James's Street, apparently displayed stumps of wax candles for sale, with the announcement that they were 'Candle-Ends from Buckingham Palace'.

Above stairs, the Queen's own immediate female entourage – the ladies in waiting (as the ladies of the Bedchamber and maids of honour were collectively called when on duty) – comprised three grades. The most senior, the ladies of the Bedchamber, who were always married and usually to peers of the realm, received an annual salary of £500. The next in rank were the eight women of the Bedchamber, who were also drawn from the aristocracy or highly respected families; and finally, the eight maids of honour, who were always the unmarried daughters or granddaughters of aristocratic families or relatives of someone who had been in service to the throne. Both these ranks received £300 a year. In addition there were, of course, the dressers and personal maids who also served the Queen, to some of whom she became extremely attached. Effectively all these women fulfilled the role of lady's companion and many of them were taken into the heart of the royal family.

One lady was always in waiting upon the Queen on a 14-day rotation; one Bedchamber woman also served for 14 days at a time, and the maids of honour served in pairs for four-week periods. All of these ladies dined in the evening at the Queen's table. The Mistress of the Robes compiled the rotas of duty for the total of 26 ladies in waiting who served the Queen.

MELBOURNE:
I thought that the Duchess would be suitable as Mistress of the Robes, Ma'am, and the Duke as you know is in the Cabinet.

VICTORIA:
She looks very elegant. Is she respectable?

MELBOURNE:
As respectable as a great lady can be, ma'am.

THE QUEEN'S LADIES, APPOINTED JULY 1837

MISTRESS OF THE ROBES:
Duchess of Sutherland

PRINCIPAL LADY OF THE BEDCHAMBER:
Marchioness of Lansdowne

LADIES OF THE BEDCHAMBER:
Marchioness of Tavistock, Countess of Charlemont, Countess of Mulgrave,
Lady Portman, Lady Lyttelton (who did not join the Household till 1838 as she
was in mourning for her husband), Lady Barham, Countess of Durham

MAIDS OF HONOUR:
Hon. Harriet Pitt, Hon. Margaret Dillon, Hon. Caroline Cocks, Hon. Miss Cavendish,
Hon. Matilda Paget (a cousin of Lord Alfred Paget), Miss Murray, Miss Harriet Lister,
Miss Spring Rice

WOMEN OF THE BEDCHAMBER:
Lady Caroline Barrington, Lady Harriet Clive, Lady Charlotte Copley, Viscountess
Forbes, Hon. Mrs Brand, Lady Gardner, Hon. Mrs G. Campbell

RESIDENT WOMAN OF THE BEDCHAMBER:
Miss Mary Davys (daughter of the Revd. Davys, Dean of Chester,
who had been Victoria's tutor at Kensington Palace)

THE LADIES OF THE BEDCHAMBER and maids of honour were invariably selected by the prime minister of the day, from families well known to him and his political friends. A code of practice, dress and behaviour among these more senior members of the Royal Household was part of the complex system of rank that had to be strictly observed. The Queen had personal control over many of her most important appointments, which were made usually on personal recommendation and after careful vetting. She was a stickler that all members of her household, from the highest to the lowest, should observe the duties of their station and share a common respect for each other.

The maids of honour in particular played a pivotal role; those first appointed by Victoria in 1837 were, like herself, very young, so much so that an amused Lord Melbourne talked of finding himself in a 'nursery' court. The Duke of Cambridge was rather more forthright, referring to one of the maids of honour out loud as *a damned pretty girl*. Young, naive and inexperienced they might be, but maids of honour had to suppress their girlish enthusiasm and toe the line. Propriety was the watchword at Buckingham Palace and Victoria was adamant that no lady was to bring her court into disrepute – hence her overreaction during the Flora Hastings affair.

Despite all the rules and regulations and the demand that they should underplay the way they looked and dressed and never go anywhere unchaperoned, young ladies of standing were eager to land a plum post at court. One such young lady, on joining the Queen, was given detailed advice by her mother on what she should expect:

> *In the first place, your first study should be to please the Queen, not by base flattery or servile cringing but by the most assiduous attention even in the merest trifles; the most rigid punctuality and obedience; not only to orders, but in being always ready at the proper time, and in the proper place [...] you must accustom yourself to sit or stand for hours without any amusement save the resources of your own thoughts [...] whatever you see, hear or think must be kept to yourself.*

~LETTER TO GEORGINA LIDDELL BLOOMFIELD
FROM HER MOTHER, FROM *REMINISCENCES
OF COURT AND DIPLOMATIC LIFE*, 1883

VICTORIA TO
MELBOURNE:
If I lose them as well
as you, then I have no
one. It will be like
Kensington again with
Mama and Sir John.
Peel does not
understand this,
but you do.

NELL HUDSON PLAYS
MISS SKERRETT

THE REAL MISS SKERRETT

- ROYAL DRESSER -

'Quite a superior person ... of the greatest discretion and straightforwardness'

···· VICTORIA ····

THE YOUNG MISS SKERRETT, apprentice dresser under Mrs Jenkins in the TV series, although fictional, owes her surname to a real-life woman, Marianne Skerrett, who was Queen Victoria's dresser for 25 years. But at this point the similarity ends.

Marianne Skerrett was a tiny little thing, 'as thin as a shred of paper' and 'comically plain' according to a relative, and she was even shorter than the Queen. She was born in 1793 the daughter of an officer who had served in the Peninsular War and owned a plantation in the West Indies. She was well educated, spoke Danish, German and French and was also extremely well read, so much so that she was forever 'recommending books all through the palace'. She was appointed Head Dresser through the recommendation of the Marchioness of Lansdowne when the Queen came to the throne in 1837, and was entrusted with the additional task of taking care of the Queen's jewellery.

In time Marianne Skerrett became one of the Queen's closest ladies, taking over a range of personal and administrative tasks beyond the mere organisation of the Queen's clothes. These included writing Queen Victoria's letters to trades people, commissioning artists and engravers, answering begging letters from old retainers and checking and paying the bills relating to the making and maintaining of the Queen's clothes. Everyone came to depend on Miss Skerrett, so much so that it was said: 'If anything goes wrong in Buckingham Palace or Windsor, whether a crowned head or a scullery maid is concerned, Miss Skerrett is always sent for to put it right.'

Marianne Skerrett – or *The Queen's Miss Skerrett*, as everyone came to call her – retired in 1862 after 25 years of loyal service, but continued to visit the Queen until her death in 1887.

VICTORIA DEMANDED A HIGH standard of education from her maids of honour. They should be able to speak, read and write French and German and also understand some Latin. Their grammar and enunciation should be 'above reproach', their voices clear, their handwriting 'ladylike'. It was essential they could sing and play the piano as well as have 'a knowledge of games, a little sketching, and of needlework'. They should be cheerful, modest and willing, and never indulge in frivolous behaviour. The way they dressed should match this, the Queen apparently having 'a great objection to smart frocks, flyaway hats, and above all, untidily dressed hair'. In the early years of her reign Victoria also expected a maid of honour to be an 'accomplished and plucky horsewoman', as they were always required to accompany her on her often extremely vigorous afternoon rides.

The most senior lady of the Bedchamber during the first few years of Victoria's reign, Lady Lyttelton, kept a watchful eye over the maids of honour. They had to apply to her for permission to do the smallest thing, and often tried to breach the very strict rules: Lady Lyttelton noted on one occasion that two maids of honour were often:

> … *very coaxy and wheedly with me… 'Lady L, mayn't I walk just for once by myself on the slopes? I know it's against the rules, but what harm can it do. We used to be allowed, but now Lord Melbourne won't let us. I'm sure we never have met anybody there.'*
>
> ~LETTER FROM LADY LYTTELTON TO HER SISTER, OCTOBER 1838

For many in the household, going out for a vigorous walk was preferable to sitting shivering in their rooms, which were underheated on the Queen's strict orders, although for others, the sheer delight of finding themselves surrounded at court by 'all the rank and fashion of London' was something of an entertainment in itself, as was being served by footmen in their crimson livery. 'Oh, in what a different sphere I am living now to what my natural one is!' young Mary Davys wrote home to her family. 'We have a good deal of fun even in a court. I cannot tell you all the little jokes, in which even the Queen joins.' In the evenings after dining with the Queen, the ladies in waiting were allowed to retire to their own rooms, but often, they would be sent for to read, sing, play the piano and join in card games in her drawing room until she retired to bed.

MARGARET CLUNIE PLAYS
THE DUCHESS OF SUTHERLAND

DUCHESS OF SUTHERLAND

- MISTRESS OF THE ROBES -

'Dearest, kindest, truest friend'

···· VICTORIA ····

HARRIET LEVESON-GOWER was born in 1806 into one of the leading Whig families of Britain, the daughter of George Howard, 6th Earl of Carlisle. Like her grandmother, Georgiana, Duchess of Devonshire, the Duchess of Sutherland was one of the most admired women of her day. She would hold the most senior female position of Mistress of the Robes on four occasions.

The Duchess was always remarked upon as being grand, in looks as well as manner. They called her 'the Great Duchess', for she moved 'like a goddess' and looked 'like a queen'. She married into considerable wealth and position in 1823 as the wife of George Granville Leveson-Gower, who inherited the title Duke of Sutherland in 1833, and became the doyenne of London high society for 40 years. But she was not just a beauty, she was also a woman of considerable intelligence and wit, a noted philanthropist and a supporter of the anti-slavery movement.

Victoria had been somewhat in awe of the Duchess and thought her 'so handsome'. The Queen could not help noticing what a close friend the Duchess was of Lord Melbourne, to the point where Victoria became a little jealous. The Duchess always sat next to him at dinner, Victoria complained in her journal, and 'made it almost impossible for him to talk to anyone else' – in other words, herself.

Mistress of the Robes was an honorary role and effectively a political appointment reflecting the Whig or Tory allegiance of a duchess's husband, so the post changed with every new government. She had charge of all the Queen's ceremonial robes and was always in attendance on her for special occasions such as Levées and Drawing Rooms, outings to the theatre, balls and official receptions as well as all state occasions – notably the Coronation and Victoria's wedding to Prince Albert.

Such was the deep bond of friendship Victoria shared with the Duchess that it prompted her refusal to dismiss her during the Bedchamber Crisis of 1839. In the end, though, the Queen was obliged to capitulate and the Duchess was forced to relinquish her post, returning to it in 1845.

ONE OF THE MOST IMPORTANT servants in Queen Victoria's household was the dresser, for they were always particularly close to her. The dressers were generally from a genteel background and treated as upper servants. They had their own bedrooms and sitting room. As such the dressers fulfilled a role that in earlier centuries had belonged to the ladies in waiting, hence the insistence on them being personally selected or recommended. Two of them waited on the Queen at any one time and they worked in conjunction with two wardrobe maids. All were unmarried. Being on duty in Victoria's private rooms, they worked long hours and sometimes suffered ill health as a result of the strain placed on them. For they not only had the care of all the Queen's wardrobe, her shoes and hats, but also the purchase of new ones and mending and alteration of existing clothes. They came under the department of the Mistress of the Robes and would liaise with her about the clothes for state ceremonials. As confidential servants, their work brought them particularly close to the Queen in her private apartments – her sitting room, bedroom and dressing room. For this reason the dresser had a position of considerable trust and responsibility.

The wardrobe maids would be expected to work with the dressers and be adept at millinery, dressmaking and hairdressing; how to clean and mend garments, clean feathers, wash lace, remove grease and stains, sort out the linen and send it to the laundry; arrange the Queen's dressing room, her toilet table and linen and take care of her jewels. Everything the Queen took off had to be looked over and, if necessary, repaired or mended either by the dresser or a wardrobe maid. Bonnets, gloves, caps and cloaks had to be inspected before Victoria put them on.

JORDAN WALKER PLAYS
LORD ALFRED PAGET

LORD ALFRED PAGET

- VICTORIA'S EQUERRY -

'Remarkably handsome in his uniform of the Blues'

···· VICTORIA ····

ALTHOUGH NEVER publicly stated, it was clear to many at the British court in the 1830s that Queen Victoria's equerry, Lord Alfred Paget, was utterly devoted to her. The fact that the Queen took a particular fancy to the dashing Lord Alfred did not go unnoticed either. At a review of the troops in September 1837, Victoria noted that he 'looked remarkably handsome in his uniform of the Blues'. There was no way that the Queen of England would or could marry a commoner, however, and Victoria herself reassured Lord M that 'it would never do' for her to marry a subject.

Lord Alfred was born in 1816, the son of Field Marshal Henry William Paget, a cavalry commander at Waterloo. The Pagets were a very distinguished family who wielded considerable power at court during the first years of Victoria's reign. The 2nd Marquis of Conyngham, who served as Lord Chamberlain, was married to a Paget and was succeeded in 1839 by Lord Alfred's father, by then Marquess of Anglesey. Both men installed their mistresses in official positions during their tenure in order to facilitate their liaisons. In addition, two of Lord Alfred's female relatives served as maids of honour and various Paget cousins held an assortment of other posts.

So ubiquitous were the Pagets at Buckingham Palace that the press referred to them as 'The Paget House Club', and certainly Lord Alfred was the next favourite in Victoria's heart after Melbourne. But he was Baroness Lehzen's pet too – she calling him 'son' and he calling her 'mother' – and the two of them were Victoria's closest allies.

The extent of Lord Alfred's devotion to his Queen became evident when in January 1839 he brought his dog to court. It was 'a fine large black dog [...] called Diver, but also sometimes Mrs Bumps', Victoria noted in her journal. 'She's a dear affectionate gentle creature and took a great liking to me.' Around her neck Mrs Bumps wore a locket containing the Queen's miniature, as did Lord Alfred himself.

Although Prince Albert deplored the profligacy of the Paget clan, and later insisted they be sent packing from court, Lord Alfred was kept on and made a captain in Prince Albert's Own Hussars. But he never quite got over seeing his adored Queen marry.

Spoke to Lord Melbourne of the set-to Lehzen had had with some of my People (servants) who had taken great liberties, and were introducing strangers into the house; of the love servants had of doing things behind one's back; of my being very strict; which Lord Melbourne said 'is the only way'. Spoke of this for some time, and Lord Melbourne was so sensible about it all; he said that the rule, which of course must be observed with my servants, namely, to take turns in waiting, was a bad training for servants; 'It's ruin to servants having nothing to do,' he said. I spoke of Chevassut (one of the Queen's young dressers), her giddiness, and I praised Jane and Anne; we agreed so well upon every point about these things; Lord Melbourne said: 'Nobody likes to do what they ought to do, in any capacity, unless they are obliged to do it'; which is very true; he said people ought to be made to work and that it was good for them.

THERE WERE ALSO, of course, equivalent male functionaries at court upon whose services the Queen would call: the lords in waiting, gentlemen ushers, equerries, footmen, pages, and grooms of the privy chamber, plus additional waiting staff for state occasions and court ceremonials and a range of military personnel attached to the royal palaces. One lord and one groom in waiting served on a 14-day rota, and one equerry on a 28-day rota, and all three of them also dined at the Queen's table.

The footmen had a special allowance for 'hair powder, bag, and silk stockings' and were given new liveries twice a year. They were there to look after guests, escort them to their rooms and see to their needs, also acting as valets to guests who had not brought their own valets with them. They decanted wine and also helped serve meals. There were also sixteen pages: six pages of the back stairs, eight pages of the presence and two state pages. The pages of the back stairs waited exclusively on the Queen; one was always on duty outside her apartments from 8 a.m. until she retired for the night; this page also served as a personal messenger and attended the Queen during most meals.

The Queen insisted on a strict hierarchy with regards to where her servants dined. The lords and ladies in waiting dined with her; members of the Royal Household who were titled had their own dining room; upper servants, including the Queen's dressers, ate in the steward's room along with the butlers, pages, messengers, housekeepers and maids of the private apartments. Lower servants ate in the servants' hall. Victoria was most particular as to the seating arrangements for her upper servants, insisting that someone who had only recently been promoted 'should not go over the heads of those confidential servants who were constantly in personal attendance on her'.

THUS THE SMOOTH WORKINGS of the machinery of the Royal Household were maintained 24 hours a day without the Queen noticing how the effort of so many contributed to her comfort. For most of the members of the Royal Household, theirs was a largely anonymous and self-effacing role. It is for this reason that so few of their names are widely known to us, despite their long years in service. Although the Palace insisted that no lord or lady who served the Queen should keep a diary of their time in waiting or confide private details about the royal family, the rule did not technically apply to letters written to their friends and families. Even so, one lady instructed her brother, 'Don't show my letters to anybody except Mama…The discretion here is extreme.' It is thanks to such letters from court, and a few diaries that were kept against the rules, that such a vivid portrait of life with Queen Victoria has come down to us.

PENGE:
Do you notice any married servants in the Royal Household?

✳✳

SKERRETT:
What about Mrs Jenkins?

✳✳

JENKINS:
What use would I have for a husband? Any fool can get married but I am chief dresser to the Queen of England. When you have been here for twenty five years, they will be calling you Mrs Skerrett too.

FERDINAND KINGSLEY PLAYS
CHARLES FRANCATELLI

MR FRANCATELLI

- CHIEF COOK AND MAÎTRE D'HÔTEL -

The palate is as capable and almost as worthy of cultivation as the eye and ear'

···· CHARLES ELME FRANCATELLI ····

T HE QUEEN'S CHEF IN the TV series is Mr Francatelli, a figure based on a real-life Anglo-Italian chef who for about two years served the Queen as Chief Cook and Maître d'Hôtel.

Charles Elme Francatelli was one of the first celebrity chefs of the Victorian era. Born in 1805 to Italian immigrant parents, he grew up in France, where he studied cookery at the Parisian College of Cooking and trained under the legendary French chef Antonin Carême, who became famous as the creator of *haute cuisine*.

In Britain, Francatelli started out working in the kitchens of the nobility – for employers including the Earl of Chesterfield, Earl of Dudley and Lord Kinnaird. In 1839 he took a job in London managing Crockford's Club and in around 1841 was engaged to cook for the Queen at Buckingham Palace. But he wasn't happy there: the working conditions and pay were poor compared with what he could command working in the exclusive London clubs, and the kitchens at Buckingham Palace at that time were still badly in need of renovation. It is also likely that the Queen and Prince Albert's preference for plain English food discouraged him in his ambitious menus. Gossip has it that the hot-headed Francatelli was dismissed for hitting a kitchen maid. Soon afterwards he took up a position at the Coventry House club on Piccadilly. In the 1850s he became chef de cuisine at the Reform Club, taking over from another celebrated French chef, Alexis Soyer.

In 1846 Francatelli published *The Modern Cook: A Practical Guide to the Culinary Art,* which was marketed under the subtitle *Recipes by Queen Victoria's Chef* and ran to 29 editions. Although it included mouth-watering menus for some of the lavish eight- and nine-course dinners he had served up for special occasions at Buckingham Palace, Francatelli was in fact an advocate of the much simpler two-course dinner, which he pioneered in his later cookery books. He also brought out a *Plain Cookery Book for the Working Classes*, full of wholesome, economical recipes for poor families. He had been heard to remark that he could 'feed a thousand families a day on the food that was wasted in London alone'.

BRODIE:
Steak and oyster!
I never had nothing
like that. Bread and
scraps if I was lucky.

❖

FRANCATELLI:
That's why one day
I am going to write a
book about my art, so
that if people can read,
they can cook.

❖

BRODIE:
Don't think Mr. Penge
would like that.

....
Opposite bottom: A page from
Francatelli's cookbook.
Left: Victoria and Albert's love of plain
food: Blanc Mange, Christmas Pudding,
Epergne and Fruit Jelly.
Opposite top: 'Her Majesty's Dinner' –
a menu cooked for Queen Victoria by
Francatelli, the Royal Confectioner.

HER MAJESTY'S DINNER. *16th August.*

(Under the control of C. Francatelli.)

Potages :

À la Cressy.   A la Tortuë.   À la Royale.

Poissons :

Le St. Pierre à la sauce Homard.
Les Gougeons frits sauce Hollandaise.

Les Filets de Soles à la ravigotte.
Le Saumon sauce aux Câpres.

Relevés :

La Pièce de Bœuf à la Flamande.
La Pâté-chaud de Pigeons à l'Anglaise.
La Noix de Veau en Bédeau.

Les Poulardes et Langue aux Choux
fleurs.

Entrées :

Les Côtelettes de Mouton à la purée d'Artichauts.
Les Boudins de Lapereaux à la Richelieu.
Les Pieds d'Agneau en Canelons farcis à l'Italiènne.
Les Filets de Poulardes à la Régence.
Les Tendons de Veau glacés à la Macédoine.
Les Petites Timbales de Nouilles à la purée de Gélinottes.

GROUPS OF FRUIT.
Frontispiece.

See page 274.

THE

ROYAL CONFE

ENGLISH AND

A PRACTICAL TREA

OF CONFE

IN ALL ITS

ORNAMENTAL CONFECTION

CHARLES EL

LATE MAÎTRE-D'HÔTEL TO HER MAJEST
"THE COOK'S GUIDE," AN

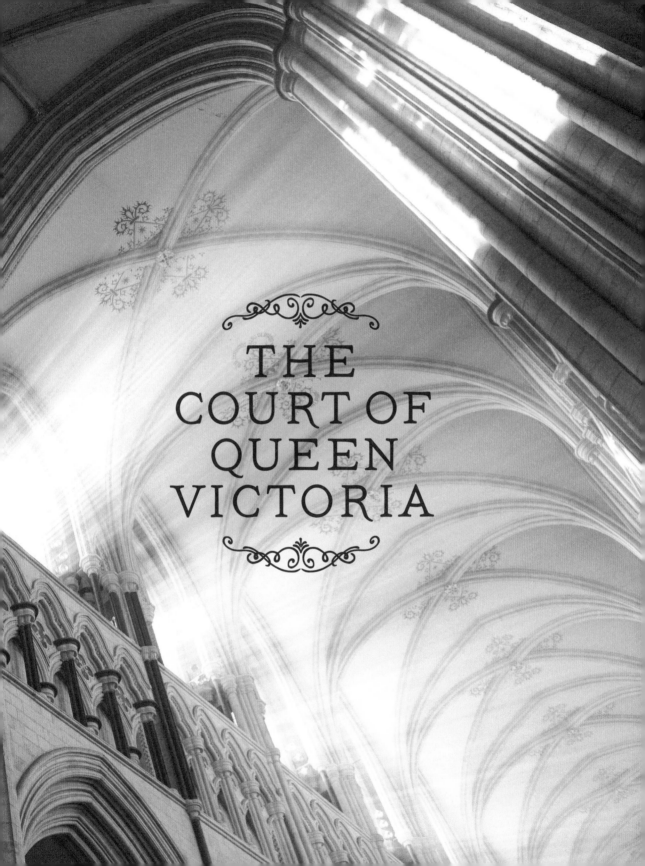

THE
COURT OF
QUEEN
VICTORIA

'I had my hand kissed nearly 3000 times!'

O N HER ACCESSION VICTORIA inherited a system of court etiquette and ceremonial that had been passed down by the Hanoverian kings, although many of the aristocracy had avoided going to court during the reign of Victoria's disreputable uncle, George IV, and court life had only begun to recover under the influence of Queen Adelaide, wife of his successor, William IV. When Victoria became Queen, an opportunity arose for the British court to be revived and reinvigorated. Victoria was young, lively and gregarious; after years of isolation she enjoyed – if not craved – company, dancing, going out to the theatre and opera, dining and after-dinner conversation.

In the first three years of her reign, she made sure she surrounded herself with people whose company she enjoyed. So much so that Uncle Leopold objected:

> *Talked of Uncle Leopold's disliking my having young people about the Court, which is too foolish; 'He thinks there is great safety in age,' said Lord M., which I said often was not the case.*
>
> ~VICTORIA'S JOURNAL, 9 OCTOBER 1839

Victoria delighted in the new sense of proprietorship that being Queen gave her. She usually conducted herself with considerable aplomb for one so young and inexperienced, as the diarist Charles Greville noted: 'In all trifling matters connected with her court and palace, she already enacts the part of Queen and Mistress as if it had been long familiar to her.'

IN THOSE FIRST HEADY months of her reign, Victoria held regular and large dinner parties at Buckingham Palace, after which there was often dancing until late into the night. When her doctor suggested that she was perhaps over-exerting herself, Victoria replied that she could never have enough such amusement. She was clearly making up for lost time:

> *I have met with so much affection, so much respect, and every act of sovereignty has been made so light, that I have not yet felt the weight of the crown… If I had a small party, I should then be called upon to exert myself to entertain my guests; but with a large one they are called upon to amuse me, and then I become personally acquainted with those who are to surround the throne.*
>
> ~ *VICTORIA QUOTED IN THE EARLY COURT OF QUEEN VICTORIA, BY CLARE JERROLD*

Private parties at Buckingham Palace were one thing; formal court occasions were quite another, however. If members of the court had hoped for some relaxation in hidebound ceremonial with Victoria's accession, they would be disappointed. She was no progressive, but rather a stickler for the same old stuffy protocols that had prevailed for the last 100 years or more. Formality ruled, as one contemporary handbook observed:

> *Since Victoria ascended the throne of these realms, the Court of Great Britain has been more scrupulously attentive to the forms and observances of official dignity than heretofore. The Queen, though so young, is strictly attentive to every particular of Court etiquette. No courtly law is violated by her, and the maintenance of Sovereign etiquette is strictly enforced and punctually attended to by all who enter the Presence Chamber.*
>
> ~ *THE ETIQUETTE OF FASHIONABLE LIFE*

MOST OF THE MAJOR COURT ceremonials took place during the London season, which ran from May to July. The two primary social occasions in the court calendar, aside from major state occasions such as the Opening of Parliament, were the Levées and Drawing Rooms held at regular intervals at St James's Palace, where the chosen few were given an opportunity to be presented to the Queen. The nominated days were advertised in the papers and there was always stiff competition among those applying for invitations.

Another typical handbook of the period was the *Court Etiquette: A Guide to Intercourse with Royal or Titled Persons, to Drawing Rooms, Levées, Courts and Audiences, The Usage of Social Life, The Formal Modes of Addressing Letters, Memorial and Petitions, The Rules of Precedence,* written by 'A Man of the World'. This and the *London Gazette* laid out the regulations for admission to court functions. Members of the nobility, their wives and daughters were of course top of the list, followed by the clergy, navy, army, physicians, barristers and the 'squirerarchy':

> *… unless there be some grave moral objection, in which case, as it has ever been the aim of the good and virtuous queen to maintain a high standard of morality within her court, the objectionable parties are rigidly excluded.*
>
> ~ COURT ETIQUETTE: A GUIDE TO INTERCOURSE
> WITH ROYAL OR TITLED PERSONS

There were firm rules about exclusion on moral grounds – no divorced people were allowed at court, nor were morganatic wives of the aristocracy. This latter ruling meant that the Queen's uncle, the Duke of Sussex – who had married his lower-ranking first and second wives against the diktats of the Royal Marriages Act – was not allowed to bring either of them to court. But in April 1840 Victoria graciously invested the Duke's second wife Cecilia with the title Duchess of Inverness, thus facilitating her return to court. As for other more lowly but hopeful loyal subjects who wished to meet their queen, the rules were clear:

> *Those of more democratic professions, such as solicitors, merchants and mechanics, have not, as a rule, that right, though wealth and connexion have recently proved an open sesame at the gates of St. James.*
>
> ~ COURT ETIQUETTE: A GUIDE TO INTERCOURSE
> WITH ROYAL OR TITLED PERSONS

THE LEVÉES, HELD BY QUEEN VICTORIA at 2 p.m. in the state apartments at St James's, were all-male affairs, providing an opportunity for aristocrats to pay their respects to her and for anyone from their ranks who had recently married or obtained a new office or professional advancement to be formally presented. They were also *de rigueur* for any foreign VIP visiting from abroad. Those being presented to the Queen for the first time had to be introduced by someone connected at court; foreign VIPs were presented by their own ambassador.

The rules of dress for gentlemen attending Levées had been set down in the late eighteenth century and nothing had changed ever since. Unlike the ladies at Drawing Rooms, men were not allowed to appear in the latest fashion. Members of the army, navy and militia had to wear full dress uniform, but those who had no official dress uniform had to wear a claret-coloured tail coat, knee breeches, an embroidered waistcoat of white or cream silk, a lace shirt with ruffles and long white silk stockings. To top it off they had to carry a sword and wear a bicorne hat with gold trimmings.

One of Queen Victoria's first important Levées was held quite soon after her accession, as she noted excitedly in her journal:

> *The Levée began immediately at ¼ p.2 and lasted till ½ p.4 without one minute's interruption. I had my hand kissed nearly 3000 times!*
> ~VICTORIA'S JOURNAL, 19 JULY 1837

Another crowded Levée came on 21 March 1838. Everyone who was anyone of course wanted to be there, as the press reported:

> *The attendance was almost unprecedented – upwards of two thousand persons. The rush and crush in the corridors equalled what may be witnessed at the pit door of a favourite London theatre. Some dignity was lost in the extraordinary pressure when, for instance, the wig of a gentleman was whisked off, and was tossed to and fro, amid laughter, before it was restored to its discomfited owner.*
> ~FROM *THE FIRST YEAR OF A SILKEN REIGN*, 1837–38
> BY ANDREW W. TUER AND CHARLES E. FAGAN, 1839

PENGE:
The Windsor uniform, your Highness, was designed by George III for members of court.

ERNEST:
I wonder if King George designed this before or after he went mad?

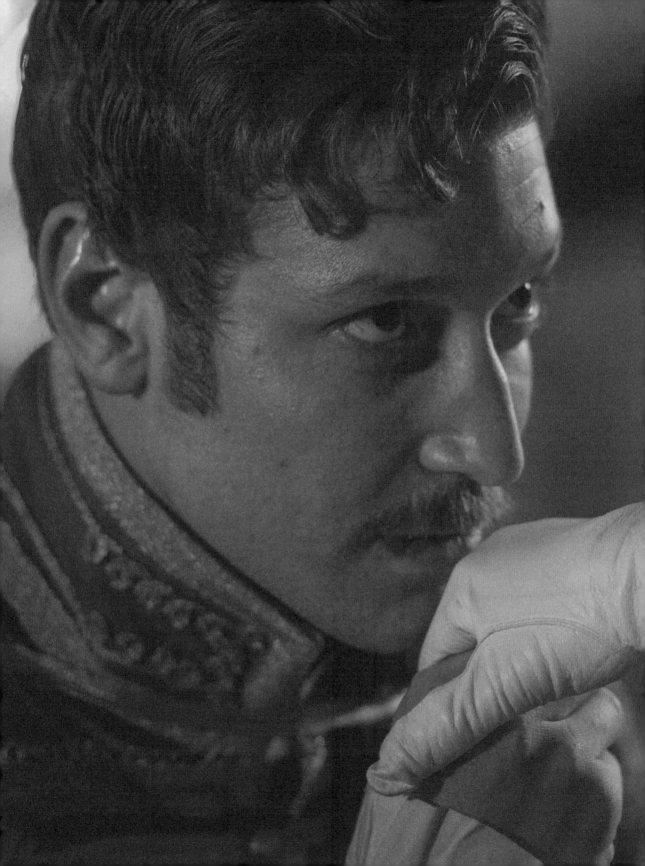

VICTORIA HANDLED THE OCCASION very well, although she had to retire briefly 'to ease my head, as my diadem (which Lord Melbourne thought "very handsome") hurt me so dreadfully'. During the hour and a half that followed, she could not but be amused at the excruciating behaviour of some of her subjects. 'The people are wonderfully awkward on being presented and never know what to do or how to kneel.'

Such uncomfortable self-consciousness is not surprising when one takes into account the strict rigmarole a gentleman had to observe, as laid out in the guides to court etiquette. The act, he was told, 'should betoken grace and homage' and be deeply respectful in manner.

> *He must kneel down on his left knee, raise his right arm, with the ungloved back of his hand uppermost, on which he receives the palm of Her Majesty's right hand; then he barely touches with his lips the back of that royal hand, which is ungloved. If he wishes to be particularly absurd and vulgar, he will kiss the hand with a loud smack, and if he be very bashful or alarmed, he will merely bow down to the hand, without the courage to touch it with his lips.*
>
> ~ *COURT ETIQUETTE: A GUIDE TO INTERCOURSE*
> *WITH ROYAL OR TITLED PERSONS*

Having managed to place a kiss on his monarch's hand with hopefully only the slightest movement of the lips, the gentleman then had to reverse away from her 'still keeping your eyes fixed upon the Queen'.

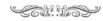

MELBOURNE:
You have quite an eye
for a uniform, Ma'am.

VICTORIA:
I am a soldier's
daughter, after all.

A T THE DRAWING ROOMS – which were only held by queens or the consorts of kings – fashionable ladies were given their chance to shine, quite literally. For, as *The Book of Fashionable Life* observed, quite apart from the gorgeous dresses, the splendid ostrich plumes and lace lappets worn on their heads, it was the 'blaze of diamonds, which are the prevailing and distinguishing ornaments of rank and beauty' and which everyone took note of.

The established regulations with regard to their dresses were far less rigid than those for the men, with one exception: court etiquette required that ladies 'should not appear in hats and feathers, or turbans and feathers, but in feathers and lappets, in conformity with the established orders'. Ordinary birds' feathers simply were not good enough: the only feathers allowed were tall and costly white ostrich plumes, which had been traditionally worn since the previous century and still prevailed, along with lace lappets and a long and unwieldy train hung from the waist. Young daughters of the aristocracy being presented for the first time often wore white, a preference that prevailed throughout the Queen's reign.

The first Drawing Rooms had been introduced in the reign of George II, when they had effectively been an occasion for his wife, Queen Caroline, to sit and play cards and gossip with other ladies. George III had held them once a week but they almost lapsed in his son's reign. It wasn't until William IV came to the throne that they were revived and held by his consort, Queen Adelaide. Although men could also attend the Drawing Rooms it was only ladies and their daughters who were presented.

....
Right: Life in Victoria's court: presentation ceremony in St James's Palace.

ICTORIA HAD HELD HER FIRST Drawing Room on 20 July 1837 in deep mourning for her uncle the King, although the quality of her 'black crape dress, richly embroidered in jet, over black silk; a train of black crape over black silk, tastefully ornamented with jet flowers' did not go unnoticed by *Blackwood's Lady's Magazine*. Her first real opportunity to enjoy all the showiness of the occasion came at her Birthday Drawing Room the following 24 May, this being 'emphatically the Drawing Room of the season'. A notice had been issued in the *London Gazette* the day before that: 'It is the particular desire of the Queen that all ladies attending her Majesty's Drawing-room should appear in dresses of British manufacture.' The reporter for the *Morning Chronicle* noted every detail on that day, including this:

> *The Queen, whose small and delicate feet are generally admired, appeared at the birthday Drawing room in so very small a pair of satin slippers, beautifully embroidered, that it is considered they could not possibly have been worn by any other lady present.*
>
> ~MORNING CHRONICLE, 25 MAY 1837

Victoria herself did not attend Drawing Rooms in state robes but usually in a red gown with the Order of the Garter ribbon over her left shoulder with the badge and an armlet with the motto of the order on her left arm, and wearing a diamond tiara. She would stand to receive her lady guests who would kneel in front of her once announced. 'The scene now becomes intensely interesting,' noted *The Book of Fashionable Life*:

> *What anxious countenances are to be seen as the line slowly advances! The silence increases as the moment of presentation approaches; the ladies prepare to drop their trains; the lappets are arranged; the cards of announcement got ready; hearts beat high; the fair debutante with graceful timidity falters for a moment; the Rubicon is passed – she is in the presence of The Queen!*
>
> ~ THE BOOK OF FASHIONABLE LIFE

21 August 1836

The band of the 1st Life Guards played during dinner. After dinner we had some vocal music. Mme. Caradori, who sings nicely but has rather a shrill and unfeeling voice, and is no Grisi; a Signor Pantaleoni, a poor imitation of the inimitable Re dei Tenori, and who, Lablache told me, 'est un jeune Italien, mais qui n'est pas grande chose' and Mr. Balfe, were the singers. The Queen told me that she had wished to have had Lablache, Ivanoff and Assandri, but as they were engaged to go on tour they could not come, which would have been delightful, quite. Balfe and Pantaleoni sung 'Voglio dirè' from L'Elissire, my favourite Duo with Lablache, and which my good Master sang so delightfully; it made me quite sad to hear it; as also Arturo dove sei', which Caradori and Pantaleoni sung – not well; and Tu vedrai, which this poor man had the boldness to try. Stayed up till 12 p.11.

VICTORIA'S JOURNAL, 21 AUGUST 1836

....
Right: Victoria aged 18 in the Royal Box at the Drury Lane Theatre.

OPERA

'I Was Very Much Amused Indeed'

···· VICTORIA ····

OF THE FEW SOCIAL ENGAGEMENTS Princess Victoria was allowed to enjoy, the one she loved most was the opera. She made regular visits with her mother during the summer seasons in London in the 1830s.

As she grew older, Victoria's passion for opera deepened, especially for those containing high drama and romance – most notably the works of the three great Italians: Bellini, Donizetti and Rossini. Her adoration of Italian opera also prompted her to learn the language. Indeed, in 1836 she even persuaded the Duchess of Kent to invite the Italian tenor Luigi Lablache to give her private lessons. Victoria adored Lablache as a father figure, and their relationship would last for 20 years.

A new and exciting generation of female singers was now replacing male castratos, and the one who caught Princess Victoria's imagination was the legendary Maria Malibran, who was noted for the high passion of her performances. When Malibran died in 1836 at the age of 28 after a sudden illness, the Princess mourned, but by now Malibran was already being supplanted by a new Italian singer, Giulia Grisi.

Victoria had first seen Grisi in her London debut in 1834 when she had been beguiled by her physical beauty, her dark eyes and hair, and her fragility and paleness, which lent a haunting vulnerability to her performances. Much to Victoria's joy, Grisi was invited to join Malibran and three male Italian opera stars – Lablache, the baritone Antonio Tamburini and the tenor Battista Rubini – in singing at a special sixteenth birthday concert organised for her in 1835 by her mother.

Victoria remained entranced by Grisi, particularly in her favourite opera – *I Puritani* – in which Grisi took a lead role. Just before coming to the throne Victoria remembered a memorable excursion to see it:

> *It was my dear I Puritani […] Grisi, Rubini, Lablache and Tamburini made their first appearance this season, and were all enthusiastically cheered […] I never saw anything look more lovely than [Grisi] did, and she sang deliciously, as did Rubini whose voice seems to get, if possible, finer each year. It is useless to add, that the singing of these 4 incomparable and unequalled artistes was, as always, perfection!* ~VICTORIA'S JOURNAL, 8 APRIL 1837

Victoria went to see this opera dozens of times. It was also the first opera she saw in the company of Prince Albert, during his visit in May 1836.

Dressed for the Ball. At a little after 10 I went into the Yellow or first Drawing-room with Ma., and all my ladies, and gentlemen, where Weippert's band was stationed. (...) At 12 p. 10 the doors were opened and I went through the Saloon into the other Ball-room next the Dining-room in which was Strauss's band. I felt a little shy in going in, but soon got over it, and went and talked to the people. (...). The rooms I must say looked beautiful, were so well lit up, and everything so well done; and all done in one day. There was no crowd at all; indeed, there might have been more people. The dining-room looked also very handsome as the supper-room. The Throne-room was arranged for the tea-room. I danced (a Quadrille of course, as I only dance quadrilles) first (in the large ball-room) with George; and 2ndly with Prince Nicholas Esterhazy; there was a valse between each quadrille; I never heard anything so beautiful in my life as Strauss's band. (...) I did not leave the ball-room till 10 m. to four!! and was in bed by 12 p. 4, – the sun shining. It was a lovely ball, so gay, so nice – and I felt so happy and so merry; I had not danced for so long and was so glad to do so again! One only regret I had – and that was, that my excellent, kind, good friend Lord Melbourne was not there. I missed him much at this my first ball; he would have been pleased I think!

VICTORIA WAS USUALLY MORE than glad to get the two-hour ritual of meeting and greeting at Levées and Drawing Rooms over and done with and, back at the Palace, indulge her love of dancing. From the late 1820s she had a dancing teacher, Madame Bourdin, who, thanks to the Duchess of Kent's patronage, ran her own Academy for Dancing in Portman Square. When she first moved into Buckingham Palace, Victoria held regular and large dinner parties, after which there was often impromptu dancing, but it was not until 10 May 1838 that she held her first state ball. As with the Drawing Rooms, people fought to get invitations, a fact which Lord M thought 'very indelicate, very pushing, very degrading'.

However, as much as Victoria loved to dance and was admired for her daintiness on her feet, it was not socially acceptable for an unmarried queen to waltz or do any dance involving intimate contact – such as being held round the waist by her male partner. This sadly limited her, until she married Prince Albert, to dancing mainly the quadrille, which enjoyed a huge resurgence in popularity in the early years of her reign. This had once been the foremost ceremonial dance at court and was similar to the cotillion, which in turn had been a version of country dance adapted for the court. The quadrille was danced in sets of four couples ranged in a line opposite each other and involved up to 16 different and often quite complicated movements called out by the Master of Ceremonies. A state ball always began with a series of quadrilles in which the Queen would partner the most important guest. At the May 1838 ball, the highly sought-after Weippert's Quadrille Band, noted for its quadrilles based on tunes from popular operas and songs, had been engaged for this, the first major ball given by Victoria as queen. Her delight in the event is evident from her diary account.

After an exhausting evening's dancing, Victoria seemed none the worse for wear the following morning and wrote to Uncle Leopold telling him, 'I have spent the happiest birthday that I have had for many years; oh how different to last year! Everybody was so kind and so friendly to me.'

By 1839, however, such had been Victoria's hectic life of dancing, staying up late and partying since her accession that Lord M had begun to worry that she might be overdoing it. Although Victoria was having a good time and was loath to give up her social life, she always listened to her prime minister. Indeed, it was becoming clear that so much play was getting in the way of her duties as monarch:

> *The Queen forgot to ask Lord Melbourne if he thought there would be any harm in her writing to the Duke of Cambridge that she really was fearful of fatiguing herself, if she went out to a party at Gloucester House on Tuesday, an Ancient Concert on Wednesday, and a ball at Northumberland House on Thursday, considering how much she had to do these last four days. If she went to the Ancient Concert on Wednesday, having besides a concert of her own here on Monday, it would be four nights of fatigue, really exhausted as the Queen is.*
>
> *But if Lord Melbourne thinks that as there are only to be English singers at the Ancient Concert, she ought to go, she could go there for one act; but she would much rather, if possible, get out of it, for it is a fatiguing time…*
>
> *As the negotiations with the Tories are quite at an end, and Lord Melbourne has been here, the Queen hopes Lord Melbourne will not object to dining with her on Sunday?*
>
> ~LETTER FROM VICTORIA TO MELBOURNE, 10 MAY 1839

Of course marriage to Albert, and the inevitable child-bearing that followed, would also soon put the dampeners on Victoria's party-loving lifestyle.

LEHZEN‡
The banquet starts at twelve, Majesty. If you don't get up now there won't be time to get ready.

THE QUEEN'S 19ᵀᴴ BIRTHDAY 1838

The illuminations in the evening were brilliant. Every club-house in St. James's Street and Pall Mall was more or less illuminated with variegated oil lamps, blazing stars, crowns, rosettes, festoons, and the initials 'V.R.' in gas or oil. In Regent Street, Messrs Dyson, the Court lacemen, displayed a transparency of Her Majesty robed and seated on the throne, with the British lion at her feet, repelling the hydra-headed demon of anarchy and confusion, the whole surrounded with the motto, 'Hail Star of Brunswick'. The most original device in the way of decoration, however, was one displayed by Mr. Grove at his fish-shop in Bond Street, where the letters composing the name of Victoria were exhibited on the shop front in red mullets, and the Order of the Garter in smelts. A stupendous cod-fish and a giant salmon undertook, for the first time, the parts of the lion and the unicorn.

~FROM *THE FIRST YEAR OF A SILKEN REIGN*, 1837–38
BY ANDREW W. TUER AND CHARLES E. FAGAN, 1839

Alophe del. et lith.

DANCING

'My Operatic and Terpsichorean feelings are pretty strong'

···· VICTORIA ····

DURING HER TEENAGE YEARS, Princess Victoria became a passionate devotee of the ballet. She not only frequently described the ballets she had seen in her journals, but also drew and painted scenes from her favourite ones in her sketchbooks and spent time creating miniature reproductions of the ballerina's costumes for her dolls.

Victoria's enthusiasm for ballet was fostered by her admiration for the leading interpreter of the European Romantic ballet, the Italian dancer Marie Taglioni, who took London by storm in the 1830s. In 1832, Taglioni created a sensation when she appeared in the new diaphanous, bell-like dancing skirt (the prototype of the tutu) at the Paris Opéra, performing what would be her most famous role – La Sylphide. Adopting the new stiffened ballet shoe, she was also one of the first ballerinas to dance on the tips of her toes and did so with a skill and grace that was transfixing.

Victoria found Taglioni's dancing magical, marvelling at how she 'flew in the air':

> *When she bounds and skips along the stage, it is quite beautiful. Quite like a fawn. And she has grace in every action. The motion of her arms and beautiful hands are so graceful, and she has such a mild sweet expression in her face.* ~VICTORIA'S JOURNAL, 2 JUNE 1835

So captivated was she by Taglioni that in 1833 she copied a costume she had worn in another ballet: 'After dinner I dressed myself up as "La Naiade", as Taglioni was dressed, with corals in my hair.'

As Victoria grew up, the opportunity to take to the dance floor herself finally arrived in May 1829. Shortly after Victoria's tenth birthday, King William IV gave a juvenile ball to honour the state visit of the girl queen Dona Maria da Glória of Portugal. At this, her first public ball, Victoria had demonstrated confident dancing skills. She repeated them at her fourteenth birthday ball at St James's Palace, in lively sets of the quadrille. Her irrepressible gaiety when dancing would be greatly inhibited by pregnancy after her marriage, but she remained a dainty dancer, and cleverly adapted the graceful glide of a ballerina in her deportment, as was often noticed.

·······
Opposite: Marie Taglioni.

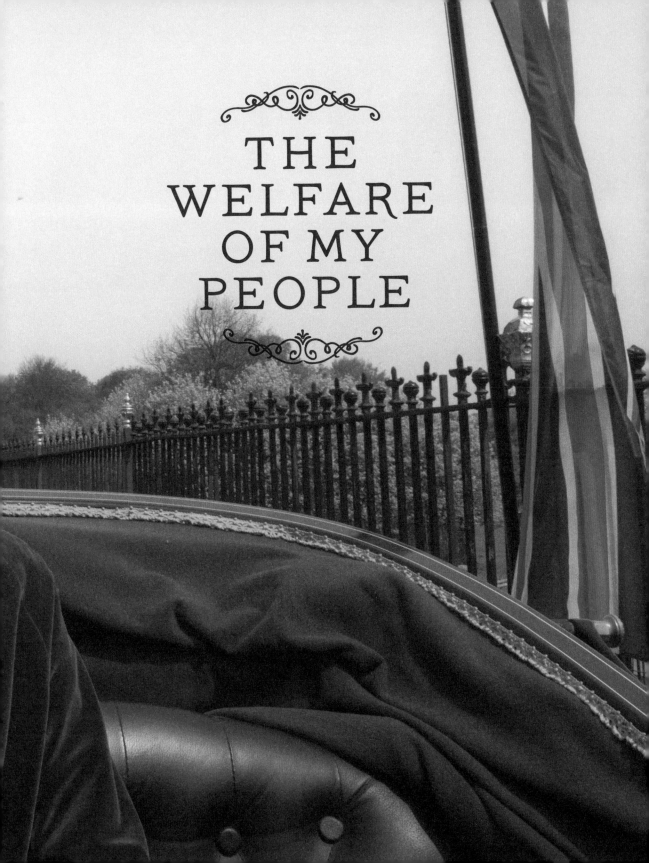

THE
WELFARE
OF MY
PEOPLE

... is ...
... Services ... a ...
fully Equal ... ...
... ... brave Soldie...
... suffering ...
... had — the pr...
... of alleviat...

So merciful ...
... ...
... my ...

'I think Oliver Twist excessively interesting and beautifully and cleverly written'

···· VICTORIA ····

WHEN VICTORIA CAME to the throne in 1837, Britain was embarking on an unprecedented period of commercial and industrial development, and with it, urban expansion. The early years of her reign witnessed the burgeoning of the manufacturing and textile industries in the north; the development of steam power supported by the growth of the iron and coal industries; the birth of the railways and steamships; reform of the mail system and the advent of the penny post; the rise of the electric telegraph and gas lighting. But it was also a time of growing public concern about the plight of the poor, who finally found a voice in the writer Charles Dickens. The widespread dissemination of his novels in cheap one- and two-penny instalments and magazine serialisations not only got people reading, but also at last brought important social issues to the fore. In novels such as the Queen's favourite, *Oliver Twist*, Dickens confronted this new nation of Victorians with the horrors of urban poverty and social deprivation. He also exposed the cruelties of the 1834 Poor Laws that had abolished outdoor relief and condemned the destitute to the inhumanity of the workhouse system.

VICTORIA HAD READ Charles Dickens's first comic novel *The Pickwick Papers* when it was serialised in 1836–37, despite the fact that her mother deeply disapproved of her reading 'light books'. But it was the novel that closely followed it that captured Victoria's imagination and that of the British public, establishing Dickens as both an important literary figure and a champion of the underclasses. Over a period of 26 months, from February 1837 to April 1839, he kept eager readers of *Oliver Twist* on tenterhooks when the novel was serialised in *Bentley's Miscellany*.

Victoria finally began reading the novel in December 1838 and found it 'excessively interesting and beautifully and cleverly written'. She discussed it on several occasions with Lord Melbourne but found it difficult to get him to engage with the novel's subject matter. Lord M, it would seem, had a pathological aversion to the realities of London's 'low life' and the 'squalid vice' that the novel depicted. When Victoria talked excitedly of the 'account of the murder of Nancy by Sikes' being 'too horrid' and that it had 'made my blood run cold', Lord M had winced, saying 'I don't like those murders…I wish to keep them away.' Victoria was very rightly indignant about the horrors that *Oliver Twist* exposed about the 'starvation in the Workhouses and Schools, where the children were not given enough to eat'. Melbourne certainly agreed that 'in many schools they give children the worst things to eat, and bad beer, to save expense', but he had found the novel much too disquieting, as Victoria recalled in her journal:

He read half of the 1st vol, at Panshanger [the home of Earl Cowper]; 'It's all among Workhouses, and Coffin Makers; and Pickpockets,' he said, 'I don't like that low debasing style; it's all slang. It's just like The Beggar's Opera; I shouldn't think it would tend to raise morals. I don't like that low debasing view of mankind.' We [Victoria and Lehzen] defended Oliver very much, but in vain; 'I don't like those things; I wish to avoid them; I don't like them in reality, and therefore I don't wish to see them represented,' he continued; that everything one read should be pure and elevating; 'Schiller, and Goethe, etc., they would have been shocked at such things.

~VICTORIA'S JOURNAL, 7 APRIL 1839

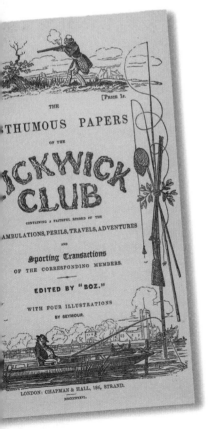

Left: Victoria read the first serialisation of *The Pickwick Papers* between 1836 and 1837.

LORD MELBOURNE MIGHT have been able to retreat to the safety and tranquillity of his home at Brocket Hall in order to avoid facing such realities, but the poor of Victorian Britain – and in particular in cities such as London – had to deal with it on an unremitting daily basis. Not only were they shackled by long working hours, low pay and poor food, but they lived in overcrowded, unsanitary living conditions, which brought with them the constant threat of disease.

Cholera in particular was rife in London during the 1830s, especially in slum areas such as the rookeries – located in the St Giles and Seven Dials area – to which young Nancy Skerrett, assistant dresser to Mrs Jenkins in the TV series, goes in Episode 6. Here, in filthy, rat-infested houses built over cesspits – for there was practically no other system of domestic sewerage and drainage at the time – there were regular cases of cholera. An outbreak in London of 1831–32 had killed 6,526 out of a population of 1.5 million. In an epidemic in 1838, 14,000 fell ill and 1,300 died. And always it was the poor in their overcrowded tenements who suffered the most.

The source of cholera infection was, as the Victorians later discovered, the stagnant River Thames, into which most of the effluent from open sewers was discharged, the germs spread by the use of shared public water pumps which drew their water from the polluted river. But in the 1830s the general belief was still that cholera was spread in the air. It was not till after a major epidemic in 1848 and the pioneering work of public health reformer Edwin Chadwick – who in 1842 published *The Sanitary Condition of the Labouring Population* – that cholera finally began to be brought under control.

SKERRETT:
Ain't these friends
of yours afraid of
the fever?

FRANCATELLI:
If you drink enough
gin, it can't touch you.

....
Right: The Seven Dials area of London,
where cholera was rife in the 1830s.

THE WORKHOUSE SYSTEM

'Work, confinement, and discipline, will deter the indolent and vicious'

···· POOR LAW COMMISSIONERS' REPORT ····

THROUGHOUT THE VICTORIAN era debate raged about the 'deserving' and 'undeserving' poor and who was worthy of support by the authorities and who was not. The consensus was that to be too free and easy in the distribution of charity to the poor would be to encourage them to rely on it. Much like debate today around the benefits system, it was thought that giving financial assistance would lead to abuse of the system; that paupers would grow lazy and be reluctant to work. Even many otherwise well-intentioned social reformers at the time considered poverty to be a matter of weakness of character in the person concerned, rather than seeing them as a victim of circumstance.

Prior to 1834 the old Poor Laws provided financial handouts to the needy in a parish, raised by taxing its middle- and upper-class inhabitants. This aroused considerable resentment, however, with taxpayers claiming that their money went to people who did not deserve it and that it encouraged the poor to have children they could not afford. In the wake of many destitute troops returning home after the Napoleonic Wars and a subsequent economic downturn in the 1830s, this old method of parish relief came under increasing strain.

The New Poor Law introduced in 1834 abolished all outdoor relief to paupers and established a workhouse system. In order to claim relief a person had to return to their home parish – no matter how far away – to do so. From now on, any individual seeking financial assistance must go into the workhouse and earn it. Once inside, workhouse administrators ensured that the experience for any claimants was as degrading and miserable as they could make it, thus discouraging inmates from entering in the first place.

As the Poor Law Commissioners' Report observed in 1834:

Into such a house none will enter voluntarily; work, confinement, and discipline, will deter the indolent and vicious; and nothing but extreme necessity will induce any to accept the comfort which must be obtained by the surrender of their free agency, and the sacrifice of their accustomed habits and gratifications.

~POOR LAW COMMISSIONERS' REPORT, 1834

If married couples applied for assistance, they were immediately separated on entering the workhouse, the men sent to break stones or to work the treadmill; the women to pick oakum. Similarly children were separated from their mothers, a fact which forced many destitute women to turn to prostitution rather than enter the workhouse. The system could not have been more punitive; as politician Benjamin Disraeli observed, 'it announced to the world that in England poverty is crime'.

Not surprisingly the poor would do anything to avoid entering the workhouse, for it felt like entering a prison. 'By many of the inmates,' wrote one contemporary observer, 'the workhouse is regarded as a sort of sepulchre in which they are entombed alive. It is assuredly the grave of all their earthly hopes.' Those with the health and strength to avoid capitulating to such incarceration may have found other ways of surviving, but for the old, the weak and the sick, the only exit from the workhouse would be in their coffins.

....
Right: 'In England poverty is crime' – dinnertime at Marylebone workhouse.
Below: 'A sort of sepulchre' – workhouse infirmary, Halifax.

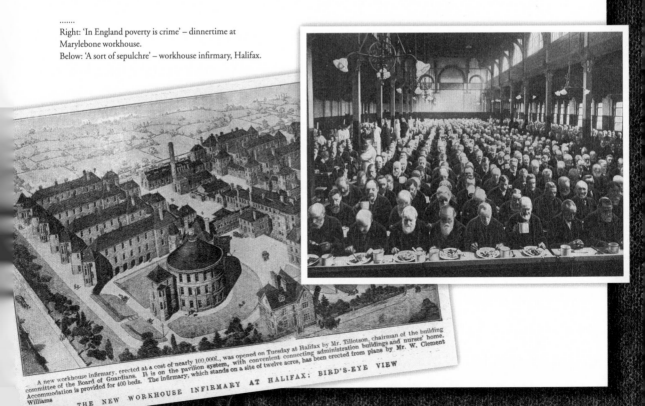

A new workhouse infirmary, erected at a cost of nearly 100,000l., was opened on Tuesday at Halifax by Mr. Tillotson, chairman of the building committee of the Board of Guardians. It is on the pavilion system, with convenient connecting administration buildings and nurses' home. Accommodation is provided for 400 beds. The infirmary, which stands on a site of twelve acres, has been erected from plans by Mr. W. Clement Williams

THE NEW WORKHOUSE INFIRMARY AT HALIFAX; BIRD'S-EYE VIEW

IF LORD MELBOURNE NEVER made any bones about his distaste for having to think about how the other half lived and his decided mistrust of social reform, then it is not surprising that he did little or nothing to arouse Victoria's social conscience during his time in office. Having lived such a sheltered life at Kensington Palace, she had remained fairly immune to the struggles of the masses until Prince Albert began to open her eyes to things after her marriage. But Victoria was not without compassion when her feelings were aroused: she did her Christian duty as any monarch should, and made charitable donations on a regular basis. She visited worthy institutions and patronised bodies set up to make a small dent in the widespread suffering of the underprivileged, but for most of the time the Queen saw nothing of the impact of poverty on ordinary people's lives.

As a 13-year-old Victoria had had a brief glimpse of the 'dark satanic mills', as William Blake would have them, of Birmingham's industrial heartland during her visit in 1832, but it was not till 1836 that she made any overt statements in her journal about the suffering of the underclasses – in this case, the plight of a family of poor gypsies camped near Claremont, whom she had got to know during her stay there that Christmas. Victoria seemed more than sensitive to the constant vilification and ostracisation of travelling people, enough to be prompted to reach for a copy of James Crabb's *Gipsies' Advocate; Or Observations on the Origin, Character, Manners, and Habits, of the English Gipsies:*

> *He beseeches and urges those who have kind hearts and Christian feelings to think of these poor wanderers, who have many good qualities and who have many good people amongst them. He says, and alas! I too well know, its truth, from experience, that whenever any poor Gipsies are encamped anywhere and crimes and robberies etc occur, it is invariably laid to their account, which is schocking [note Victoria's Germanic spelling of the word]; and if they are always looked upon as vagabond, how can they become good people. I trust in Heaven that the day may come when I may do something for these poor people.*
>
> ~VICTORIA'S JOURNAL, 29 DECEMBER 1836

....
Right: Gypsy women sketched by Victoria.

CLOSER TO HOME, ONE of Victoria's first charitable interests while still a princess had been the Children's Friend Society. It had been founded in 1830 by Edward Brenton, a former naval officer and philanthropist, to rescue homeless and destitute children from the streets, give them a training and place them in suitable employment – which in the main involved sending them overseas to work in the colonies. Brenton had established a home for boys in Hackney and another for girls in Chiswick, which, thanks to Victoria's patronage, later became known as the Royal Victoria Asylum. It is from here that the show's Nancy Skerrett has been sent to work at the Palace.

Princess Victoria had visited the Chiswick home in 1836:

It is a most interesting and delightful establishment […] It is for poor vagrant girls, who are received under the age of 15; and Miss Murray says that they have never had a girl six months who did not become a perfectly good child. I forget how young they receive children, but there are girls in all, and they are divided, a few being in an infant school upstairs.

When they have become quite good, and can read, write and do work of all kinds necessary for a house, they are sent abroad, mostly to the Cape of Good Hope, where they are apprenticed and become excellent servants. Miss Murray told us many curious stories of the depraved and wretched state in which many arrive, and how soon they become reformed and good. There is one little girl in particular, a very pretty black-eyed girl, 11 years old, called Ellen Ford, who was received two month ago, from Newgate, and who boasted she could steal and tell lies better than anybody. She had been but two or three days in the school, and she got over three high walls, and stole a sheet; she was caught and brought back again.

Miss Murray spoke to her, and found that the poor girl had no idea whatever of a God, and had a drunken father, a low Irishman. This man had lost his first wife and married again, and this step-mother taught the girl nothing but stealing and lying. Miss Murray told her of God, and spoke to her very seriously. The girl was put in solitary confinement for that night and was taken out the next morning; and ever since she has been a perfectly good girl. There are many cases of the same sort, which Miss Murray said she could relate.

~VICTORIA'S JOURNAL, 3 AUGUST 1836

VICTORIA'S UNDERSTANDABLY LIMITED view of the work at Chiswick did not, however, square with how things were carried out in practice. Life for some of the girls after leaving the Institute and being sent to the Colonies was grim and soon accusations of child trafficking and slave labour – of children being starved and beaten – were being levelled at the Children's Friend Society. Such negative reports greatly undermined its reputation and in 1840 a government inquiry demanded an improvement in standards. But by now donations had melted away and the following year the society disbanded. For the destitute children who no longer received the society's assistance, just as for the weak and the old and infirm, the only recourse when charity failed them was a life of crime or the workhouse.

WEST FRONT, OR PRINCIPAL ENTRANCE OF THE LONDON WORKHOUSE, BISHOPSGATE STREET.

WITH THE STEWARDS SIDE, OR INTERNAL PART OF THE SAME STRUCTURE.

London, Published 2 January 1814 by Robert Wilkinson, 58, Cornhill, 1818.

....
Left: 'When charity failed ...' – London Workhouse, Bishopsgate Street.

THE ROOKERIES
OF ST GILES
AND SEVEN DIALS

'Where misery clings to misery for a little warmth'
···· THOMAS MILLER ····

SEVEN DIALS, WHERE Nancy Skerrett ventures in Episode 6 and which was made famous in the writings of Charles Dickens, was a notorious area of slum dwellings on the edge of London's Covent Garden. Together with the neighbouring parish of St Giles, it was a maze of streets, courts, lanes and alleys – a place of prostitution, crime, destitution and despair. As one contemporary observer, Thomas Miller, put it in his book *Picturesque Sketches of London* (1852), it was a place where 'misery clings to misery for a little warmth, and want and disease lie down side-by-side and groan together'.

Charles Dickens had taken many night-time walks round these two areas when gathering material for his *Sketches by Boz* of 1835 and drew on his knowledge to create Fagin's and Bill Sikes's haunts in *Oliver Twist*. A contemporary magazine account gives a vivid sense of what life was like there:

> Who that has passed St Giles's on the way to the City [...] but has caught a glimpse, through some narrow opening, of its squalid habitations, and wretched and ruffianly occupants! Who but must have been struck with amazement, that such a huge receptacle of vice and crime should be allowed to exist in the very heart of the metropolis, like an ulcerated spot, capable of tainting the whole system.
>
> Entering a narrow street, guarded by posts and crossbars, a few steps from the crowded thoroughfare brought you into a frightful region, the refuge, it was easy to perceive, of half the lawless characters infesting the metropolis. The coarsest ribaldry assailed your ears, and noisome odours afflicted your sense of smell. As you advance, picking your way through kennels flowing with filth, or over putrescent heaps of rubbish and oyster-shells, all the repulsive and hideous features of the place were displayed before you. There was something savagely picturesque in the aspect of the place, but its features were too loathsome to be regarded with any other feeling than disgust. The houses looked as sordid, and as thickly

crusted with the leprosy of vice as their tenants […] Horrible habitations they were, in truth. Many of them were without windows, and where the frames were left, brown paper or tin supplied the place of glass; some even wanted doors, and no effort was made to conceal the squalor within. On the contrary, it seemed to be intruded on observation. Miserable rooms almost destitute: floors and walls caked with dirt, or decked with coarse flaring prints; shameless and abandoned looking women; children without shoes and stockings, and with scarcely a rag to their backs; these were the chief objects that met the view […] So thickly inhabited were these wretched dwellings, that every chamber, from garret to cellar, swarmed with inmates. As to the cellars, they looked like dismal caverns, which a wild beast would shun. Clothes-lines were hung from house to house, festooned with every kind of garments. Out of the main street branched several alleys and passages, all displaying the same degree of misery, or, if possible, worse, and teeming with occupants […] It was impossible to move a step without insult or annoyance. Every human being seemed brutalised and degraded; and the women appeared utterly lost to decency, and made the street ring with their cries, their quarrels, and their imprecations. It was a positive relief to escape from this hot-bed of crime to the world without, and breathe a purer atmosphere. ~AINSWORTH'S MAGAZINE, NOVEMBER 1844

....
Below: 'Squalid habitations' – Rookery at St Giles, London, 1849.

WHILE PHILANTHROPISTS AND social campaigners were
raising their voices in the fight to improve the lot of the
underprivileged, the British public could at least take pride in some
of the advances in technology that took place during the early years
of Victoria's reign. Undoubtedly one of the greatest changes to
the life of the nation was the development of steam power, which
ushered in the design and construction of the first steam locomotives
and steamships. In April 1838 the *Great Western* – a paddle steamer
designed by Isambard Kingdom Brunel and which operated out
of Bristol – and the London-based steamship the *Sirius* both made
the first Atlantic steam crossing in fifteen days. But it was on land
where the most important changes came.

The engineer George Stephenson's steam locomotive had first
been tried out on the Stockton & Darlington line in 1825, but it was
not until the Liverpool & Manchester line was opened five years later,
offering the first passenger service, that the railway age took its first
tentative steps, marking a transition from the old coaching system.
In July 1837 a 25-mile line of rail track out of a new station at Euston
was opened, as the first stage of a link from the capital to Birmingham.
Building the new network of railways was, however, an extremely
expensive exercise. The cost of levelling the ground, of excavating
tunnels and laying the rails, averaged a colossal £50,080 per mile and
it was not until September 1838 that the Grand Junction Railway
Company opened the full 112-mile passenger route to Birmingham.
It meant that many people were able to travel into London by rail
to witness the Queen's Coronation procession in 1838.

It would not be until the 'railway mania' of the 1840s that the rail network was sufficiently developed as a means of efficiently transporting fee-paying passengers. This began with the Great Western Railways offering a link between London and Bristol in 1841, but already in the 1830s it had done much to offer an accelerated postal service that would soon be taking business from the old traditional mail coaches. The Birmingham to Liverpool railway now offered a daily mail service between London and Holyhead, which took 26 hours instead of several days by the old coaching methods. This development came hand in hand with a reformed and revitalised postal service that would greatly reduce the length of time needed for any letter to reach its destination.

In November 1839 Queen Victoria was delighted to be shown examples of the new adhesive penny postage stamp bearing her image – the first of its kind anywhere in the world. It was the culmination of several years of lobbying and reports calling for postal reform championed by the educator and social reformer Rowland Hill. Hill argued that the old system was costly and laborious and suggested that letters be carried with a prepaid stamp on them, which would do away with the letter being paid for by its recipient, when delivered.

Victoria certainly had hopes of the service being of great benefit to the nation, as she had stated when she prorogued Parliament that August:

> *I trust that the Act [...] will be a relief and encouragement to trade; and that, by facilitating intercourse and correspondence, it will be productive of much social advantage and improvement [...] that the beneficial effects of this measure will be felt throughout all classes of the community.*
>
> ~VICTORIA AT THE PROROGATION OF PARLIAMENT, 27 AUGUST 1839

VICTORIA:
And my likeness will
be on every letter?

❋❋

ROWLAND HILL:
Yes Ma'am. This is the
Royal Mail, after all.

....
Top right: Penny Red postage stamp, 1841.
Right: Two Penny (or Two Pence) Blue postage stamp, 1840s.

T HE RAPID EXPANSION of British industry in the 1830s had brought with it an inevitable growth in the urban labour force, with a great movement of labour from the countryside into the cities. As a result rural areas had been suffering economic depression, and unrest was provoked by the introduction of mechanisation that saw many agricultural labourers put out of work. There was growing dissent too about the corn laws which fixed the price of flour and pushed up the price of bread. Workers were struggling to feed their families, but they were also, at last, finding a political voice and making increasingly forceful demands for control of their working hours and pay, for trade unions and the right to the vote.

Many of those now demanding sweeping change to the antiquated and corrupt electoral system had been bitterly disappointed by the 1832 Reform Act, which had failed to extend the franchise beyond about 18 per cent of the adult male population and which had given no rights to the non-property-owning labouring classes.

In May 1838, at a meeting held in Glasgow, a People's Charter was drawn up outlining six key demands: for universal suffrage, vote by ballot, annual parliaments, payment of MPs; abolition of the property qualification and equal electoral districts. The charter made its aspirations clear in its opening statement:

We hold it to be an axiom in politics, that self-government by representation is the only just foundation of political power – the only true basis of constitutional rights – the only legitimate parent of good laws; – and we hold it as an indubitable truth, that all government which is based on any other foundation, has a perpetual tendency to degenerate into anarchy or despotism, or to beget class and wealth idolatry on the one hand, poverty and misery on the other.

–THE PEOPLE'S CHARTER, MAY 1838

....
Opposite right: The Six Points of the People's Charter, Glasgow, 1838.
Below right: Chartist Riot at Newport, 4 November 1839.

The Six Points

OF THE

PEOPLE'S

CHARTER.

1. A VOTE for every man twenty-one years of age, of sound mind, and not undergoing punishment for crime.

2. THE BALLOT.—To protect the elector in the exercise of his vote.

3. No PROPERTY QUALIFICATION for Members of Parliament —thus enabling the constituencies to return the man of their choice, be he rich or poor.

4. PAYMENT OF MEMBERS, thus enabling an honest trades-man, working man, or other person, to serve a constituency, when taken from his business to attend to the interests of the country.

5. EQUAL CONSTITUENCIES, securing the same amount of representation for the same number of electors, instead of allowing small constituencies to swamp the votes of large ones.

6. ANNUAL PARLIAMENTS, thus presenting the most effectual check to bribery and intimidation, since though a constituency might be bought once in seven years (even with the ballot), no purse could buy a constituency (under a system of universal suffrage) in each ensuing twelvemonth; and since members, when elected for a year only, would not be able to defy and betray their constituents as now.

FROM THIS CHARTER sprang the Chartist movement that would come to dominate politics during the first two decades of Victoria's reign and would lead to a period of political discontent and public protest. One of the first serious manifestations of this came in 1839, with the Newport Rising. From the outset, Victoria's government and the press played down this grassroots, working-class surge of protest as nothing more than 'Disturbances'. But it was much more serious than that. On 4 November 1839, up to 10,000 Welsh miners and ironworkers marched in protest at the arrest of a Welsh Chartist leader on a charge of unlawful assembly. A few of the insurgents had pistols and swords but most were armed with pikes, farm implements and any offensive weapons they could lay their hands on. The authorities had been tipped off about the route of the march through Newport and had secreted about 32 troops of the 45th Nottinghamshire regiment and several special constables in the Westgate Hotel. As the marchers headed their way, they were fired on from inside the hotel. About 24 marchers were killed and many more wounded.

Horrified by this act of insurrection, as she saw it, Victoria questioned what had prompted it. 'You always tell me the British are not a revolutionary people,' she told Melbourne, who explained that the threat of Chartism had been brewing for some time and 'it must be expected to break out at last'. Naturally enough, Victoria was impressed by the bravery of the commanding officer, Lieutenant Grey, who had been hugely outnumbered and praised his 'very gallant conduct at Newport with only 28 men against 4000 Chartists'. The three ringleaders of the march, who had hoped their protest would trigger a nationwide insurrection, were arrested and tried in Monmouth on 31 December. After a seven-day trial, in January 1840 they were found guilty of high treason. Surprisingly for one so young and impressionable, Victoria did not seem the least fazed by the sentence that was handed down to them, noting in her journal:

Talked of Frost, Williams, and Jones being pronounced guilty of Treason, and of the sentence in the papers being just like in former times – to be hanged, drawn and quartered.

~VICTORIA'S JOURNAL, 17 JANUARY 1840

MELBOURNE:
Some Chartists believe
that women should
have the vote.

VICTORIA:
Now you
are teasing me.

THERE WAS CONSIDERABLE protest, however, at the prospect of such a barbaric penalty being carried out, and, after concerted petitioning, the sentence was commuted to transportation for life to Van Diemen's Land. Victoria of course took the side of law and order and duly knighted the Mayor of Newport, who she considered had:

…distinguished himself so much in that riot of the Chartists. […] he is a very timid, modest man, and was very happy when I told him orally how exceedingly satisfied I am with his conduct. The officers have been rewarded too.

~LETTER FROM VICTORIA TO ALBERT, 8 DECEMBER 1839

ALTHOUGH THE GROWING voice of Chartism would resurface with increasing violence throughout the 1840s, Queen Victoria herself had already become the target of acts of political protest and violence from the moment of her accession. Some at the time were labelled as 'assassination attempts' by the hysterical British press, but in the main they were acts by mentally unstable attention seekers with no real intention to kill.

On 10 June 1840 Edward Oxford, an 18-year-old public house pot boy from Birmingham, had pulled a pistol from under each armpit and fired two shots at Victoria and Albert, when they were travelling one evening in an open carriage up London's Constitution Hill.

Victoria was four months pregnant at the time and Prince Albert's alarm had been considerable:

My chief anxiety was lest the fright should have been injurious to Victoria in her present state. I seized Victoria's hands, and asked if the fright had not shaken her, but she laughed at the thing. I then looked again at the man, who was still standing in the same place, his arms crossed, and a pistol in each hand.

~LETTER FROM ALBERT TO HIS GRANDMOTHER,
THE DOWAGER DUCHESS OF GOTHA, 11 JUNE 1840

XFORD WAS QUICKLY apprehended by bystanders, and openly admitted, 'It was me that did it,' muttering that he didn't think the country should be ruled by a queen. Albert had found his attitude 'so affected and theatrical it quite amused me'. Victoria, who had been looking the other way, had displayed her characteristic sang-froid, noting in her journal that when Oxford was interrogated at Newgate, he 'had not appeared to be in the least mad; and was very impudent and flippant during the examination'.

Whether or not Oxford had acted alone or what his precise intention had been was never established, although Lord Melbourne informed Victoria that 'letters about a secret society had been found at Oxford's house'. This turned out to be some kind of fictitious military society that Oxford had concocted and to which he had given the name Young England. For a brief while it was suggested that this 'society' was a reactionary, ultra-Tory group bent on undermining Victoria's rule and masterminded by the resident royal bogeyman, the Duke of Cumberland.

There was some question as to how Oxford had gained possession of the two decorative (rather than functional) silver-mounted pistols he had used. There was also considerable disagreement as to whether his guns had any bullets or merely, as Oxford claimed, discharged gunpowder – for no bullets were found at the scene.

For Oxford's trial, the prosecution had prepared a mass of evidence and witness statements, which demonstrated that he was of unsound mind, the son of an alcoholic father and grandfather, and that his mother was the victim of repeated domestic violence. Medical witnesses all concurred that Oxford was mentally disturbed and he was declared guilty but insane and confined to a lunatic asylum, at Her Majesty's Pleasure. Eventually Oxford was transferred to Broadmoor, from where he was released in 1867 before emigrating to Australia.

Victoria's displayed courage was a great boost to her public image. Lord M had told her 'with tears in his eyes' that the public outpouring of sympathy was 'very deep'. The following day they went out for their afternoon drive as usual. It was a shrewd move and one that guaranteed endless reiterations of public gratitude and thanksgiving for the Queen's 'escape from assassination'. It was an important moment too in the history of the British monarchy, for it marked the transition to a more popular style of monarchy that engaged with the British public.

THE ANTI-SLAVERY
CONVENTION

'A cause so sacred'

···· SOCIETY FOR THE EXTINCTION OF THE SLAVE TRAFFIC ····
···· AND THE CIVILISATION OF AFRICA ····

I N 1833 SLAVERY HAD been brought to an end by an act of Parliament, freeing some 800,000 slaves throughout the British Empire, but the practice persisted still in America and many other parts of the world. In June 1840 a coming together of all the major figures in the worldwide anti-slavery movement was organised in London. Taking place between 12 and 23 June, the World Anti-Slavery Convention held at London's Exeter Hall – a noted venue used for philanthropic and religious meetings – was the work of leading British and American Quaker reformers. It was attended – after considerable debate about their admittance – by seven female delegates, the first time women were admitted to any such convention.

Prince Albert's passionate support of the anti-slavery movement provided an ideal opportunity for him to make his debut in British public life, and set the tone of his own social and political concerns. On 1 June, just prior to the Anti-Slavery Convention, he agreed to accept the office of President and take the chair at the anniversary meeting of the Society for the Extinction of the Slave Traffic and the Civilisation of Africa at Exeter Hall. The organisers were delighted that the Prince should identify himself 'with a cause so sacred, which would be the expressive proof […] of the disposition of the Prince to render his distinguished station subservient to the great objects of humanity and benevolence'.

Once word got out that the Prince was to make an appearance, there was a rush by the great and the good for tickets, so much so that a crowded and animated Exeter Hall 'looked like the House of Lords in session'. Albert had carefully prepared his speech in German and translated it with Victoria's help; he also nervously rehearsed it with her before setting off to his audience of 4,000.

Upon his arrival, the Prince was greeted by thunderous applause and 'proceeded with great distinctness, and with a very slight foreign accent, to open the business of the day':

1 June 1840

I have been invited to preside at the meeting of this society from a conviction of its paramount importance to the great interests of humanity and justice. (Cheers) I deeply regret that the benevolent and persevering exertions of England to abolish that atrocious traffic in human being, at once the desolation of Africa and the blackest stain upon civilised Europe, have not yet led to any satisfactory conclusion. But I sincerely trust that this great country will not relax in its efforts until it has finally and for ever put an end to a state of things so repugnant to the spirit of Christianity, and to the best feelings of our nature. (Tremendous applause) Let us, therefore, trust that Providence will prosper our exertions in so just a cause, and that under the auspices of our Queen and her Government we may at a distant period be rewarded by the accomplishment of the great and humane object for the promotion of which we have this day met. (Loud and long-continued cheers).

ALBERT'S SPEECH AT THE ANNIVERSARY MEETING OF THE SOCIETY FOR THE EXTINCTION
OF THE SLAVE TRAFFIC AND THE CIVILISATION OF AFRICA, EXETER HALL

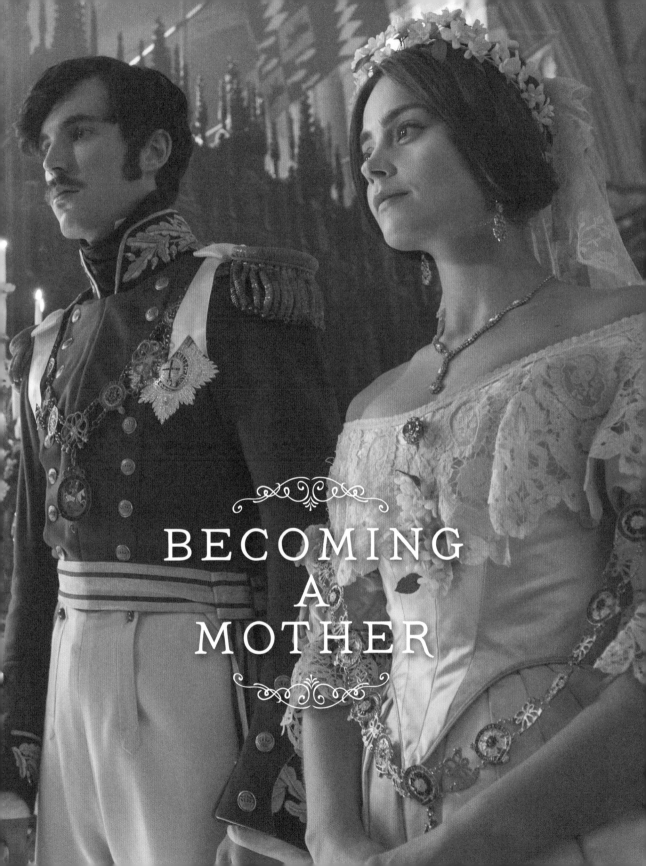

BECOMING
A
MOTHER

'How can I ever be thankful enough to have such a Husband!'

···· VICTORIA ····

WHEN QUEEN VICTORIA married Prince Albert of Saxe-Coburg-Gotha on 10 February 1840, it was the first wedding of a reigning queen to take place in Britain since 1554, when Queen Mary I had married Philip II of Spain. Victoria's grandfather George III had been the last reigning king to marry, in 1761, but his union with Charlotte of Mecklenburg-Strelitz had been very much one of dynastic expediency. Things were very different this time; Britain's pretty little queen was marrying for love. When she had been asked whether, as monarch, she wished to omit the promise to obey from the service, she had been most insistent: 'I wish to be married as a woman, not as a Queen.'

Up until 1840 royal marriages had been held in the evening in front of a few select guests, but for this one the timing was changed in order to make it possible for ordinary people to see something of the procession. At first Victoria had wondered whether it might not be better to hold the wedding in St George's Chapel at Windsor, but it was decided that the people of London could not be denied the chance of witnessing the event. Privately, she had other reasons for opting for the smaller venue of St James's. Still seething over the Bedchamber Crisis, and angry about the antipathy towards Albert in Parliament, she had struck the names of all but five loyal Tories off the guest list, making an exception of the Duke of Wellington, for whom she had a particular affection. 'It is MY marriage,' she had told Lord M, 'and I will only have those who can sympathise with me.'

VICTORIA AND ALBERT'S wedding day dawned cold, wet and foggy. Waking in her room at Buckingham Palace, Victoria's first thought was that this was 'the last time I slept alone'. Defying convention, she had a brief, private meeting with Albert before being dressed in her bridal gown.

Outside on the streets, her eager subjects had been gathering since daybreak all along the route from Buckingham Palace to St James's, just as they had crowded the capital for Victoria's Coronation a year and a half previously. By 9 a.m. 'the crowd between the palaces was very considerable; and at eleven o'clock, the pressure was distressing', reported journalist John Timbs, but they remained cheerful. Once again, every possible vantage point was occupied; young people climbed up into the trees along the route to get a better view and some were injured when the branches they were sitting on broke under their weight. Then, after a long cold wait, came 'the premonitory sounds of the Queen's departure from Buckingham Palace':

> *The noise of many drums, the brazen throats of signal guns, and the clang of martial trumpets had scarcely ceased their loud announcement, when the State carriage in which Her Majesty rode issued from the marble portal. The troops presented arms as the Queen passed; the bands performed the national anthem.*
>
> *– BRISTOL TIMES AND MIRROR, FEBRUARY 1840*

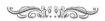

MELBOURNE:
Such crowds gathering for your wedding, Ma'am. I think you should ride from the Chapel Royal to the Palace in an open carriage. I fancy it would mean something to the Prince to hear the crowds cheering for him.

A T ST JAMES'S EVERY possible space in the Chapel Royal was crammed with chairs, its walls were festooned in red velvet and a scarlet Brussels carpet had been specially laid on the floor. A profusion of royal gold plate glittered on the altar, in front of which four gilded chairs with footstools had been placed. Five hundred guests had been squeezed in tight for the ceremony two hours beforehand and spent 'two mortal hours of shivering' until the ceremony began at one.

Prince Albert, flanked by his father and brother, looked very handsome standing at the altar in his uniform of a British field marshal with its fitted red swallow-tail jacket and white knee breeches that flattered his striking physique. He wore the insignia of the Order of the Garter set in precious stones attached to two white satin rosettes on his right shoulder, and the Garter itself tied round his knee.

To a flourish of trumpets Lord Melbourne preceded the Queen down the aisle, carrying the Sword of State. Victoria looked pale and anxious but excited, in a wedding gown of white satin with deep lace flounces and a matching lace veil and a simple wreath of orange blossoms round her head. The satin train hanging from her waist was carried by eight bridesmaids, two of whom were Paget cousins of Victoria's favourite, Lord Alfred. Albert had insisted they be unmarried young women of spotless character. Wearing white roses in their hair and simple white tulle dresses, made from Victoria's own sketches, 'they looked like village girls, among all the gorgeous colours and jewels that surrounded them,' remarked Lady Lyttelton. Unfortunately, the Queen's train was a little short and, as one of the bridesmaids recalled, 'we were all huddled together, and scrambled rather than walked along, kicking each other's heels, and treading on each other's gowns.'

As she processed to the altar, Victoria was accompanied by her mother, in a white satin dress embroidered in silver, and a splendid-looking Duchess of Sutherland, who wore a gown of pink moiré, embroidered in a pattern of seaweed and shells. Towering over them all stood her uncle, the Duke of Sussex, who was to give her away; ever the eccentric, he chose to wear a black skull-cap, having complained that his head would get cold otherwise.

VICTORIA:
I think I would like
my wedding dress
to be white.

THE WEDDING DRESS

WHEN VICTORIA FIRST discussed her wedding clothes with Lord M, she insisted that she did not wish to wear her usual cumbersome state robes. 'Oh, no!' he concurred, 'I should think not, much better wear white.' Until then it had not been traditional for a royal – or any other bride – to wear white, and one of Victoria's reasons for choosing this colour was so that she might be more visible to her people when she rode in her carriage to St James's Palace. In doing so, she would of course set a trend. Prior to this, white material was little used because it was expensive to produce and hard to keep clean. It was certainly not a practical choice for poorer brides, who, in the main, wore coloured dresses at their weddings.

At the time, Victoria was criticised for choosing white, for girls and unmarried women often wore white as mourning. People also complained about her refusal to wear more elaborate, traditional dress – no velvet or ermine or fancy tiara. But Victoria always made her own choices and stubbornly stuck to them.

She was insistent right from the start that her dress should be made of British manufactured fabrics, in this case white silk satin made in Spitalfields, with a broad flounce of Honiton lace from Devon overlaying the skirt and as flounces on the sleeves. The dress was decorated with orange blossom flowers (a symbol of fertility), and complemented by a necklace and large drop earrings of Turkish diamonds. On her bosom Victoria wore a blue sapphire brooch that Albert had given her as a wedding present. Her simple bouquet contained sprigs of myrtle – the symbol of everlasting love.

The Honiton lace for the Queen's dress and veil was in fact not made in Honiton but in the small Devonshire village of Beer. Jane Bidney, a lacemaker in St James's and a native of Beer, was sent from London to supervise the team of 200 women who worked on the lace. The £460 paid for the lace (more than £20,000 today) certainly came at the right time for the declining trade; according to the press, had the lacemakers in Beer not received this commission, 'they would have been destitute during the winter'.

The pattern for the lace was designed by Scottish artist William Dyce; the dress was the work of court dressmaker Mrs Mary Bettans, who was so anxious that the dress should be unique that after it had been made she destroyed the patterns. Victoria was so pleased with the lace that she sent the makers money so they could hold a celebratory tea party on the day of her wedding.

....
Opposite: Victoria in her wedding dress in 1840.

THE CEREMONY TOUCHED THE heart of many present, including the wife of the American ambassador:

Both made the responses very audibly, but her tones, tho' soft and low, were yet so perfectly distinct that every one in the chapel heard her vow to love, honor & obey; and when he promised to love and cherish her, she turned her sweet and innocent looks upon him with an expression that brought tears into every eye that saw it.

~LETTER FROM SALLIE STEVENSON, WIFE OF
THE AMERICAN AMBASSADOR, 19 FEBRUARY 1840

ALBERT:
You shall not lose me.
My desire for you shall
never fail. A love like
ours could burn
down a city.

One lady present had thought the Prince 'appeared awkward from embarrassment and was a good deal perplexed and agitated in his response'; by the end of the service, as Lady Lyttelton noted, the Queen's eyes were 'much swoln with tears, but great happiness in her face; and her look of confidence and comfort at the Prince as they walked away as man and wife was very pretty to see'.

Victoria's own account, written in her journal later, suffered perhaps from the emotional overload of the day and for once she seemed lost for words:

The Ceremony was very imposing, and fine and simple, and I think ought to make an everlasting impression on every one who promises at the Altar to keep what he or she promises. Dearest Albert repeated everything very distinctly. I felt so happy when the ring was put on, and by Albert. ~VICTORIA'S JOURNAL, 10 FEBRUARY 1840

As for Mama, she may have been present throughout the day, but Victoria was so absorbed by Albert that she paid her little attention. The Duchess of Kent's last intimate act as a mother had been to place the bouquet of orange blossoms in her daughter's hands as she prepared for the wedding. Thereafter, she had been out of the frame. Throughout the service, to those who even noticed her presence, she had seemed disconsolate and distressed; the sense of alienation from a daughter who had already withdrawn from her was profound. With her closest lady in waiting, Lady Flora Hastings, dead and her trusted Conroy out of the country, the Duchess now struck a lonely, pathetic figure.

HER MAJESTY'S BRIDAL CAKE.

THE WEDDING CAKE

THE ELABORATE CAKE made for the Queen's wedding to Prince Albert in February 1840 was not made by Victoria's chef Francatelli as depicted in the TV series, but was in fact the creation of John Chichester Mawditt, First Yeoman of the Confectionery to Her Majesty (to give him his full title), who was based at Buckingham Palace. It formed a most splendid centrepiece to the wedding breakfast and by all accounts was the most luxurious cake ever made there, coming in at 300 pounds in weight and costing 100 guineas.

The workmanship that went into the cake's creation was considerable – as one contemporary account observed:

> *It far exceeded all its rivals and indeed any bride-cake ever seen, in tasteful and appropriate design, as in dimensions. It was more than nine feet in circumference, by 16 inches deep; and upon this solid base a fine super-structure was erected. Two pedestals rose from the plateau of the cake, the upper one supporting another plateau, on which stood Britannia gazing upon the royal pair, who were in the act of pledging their vows. At their feet were two turtle doves, emblems of love and purity, and a dog, representing constancy of attachment. A little lower down, Cupid was seen writing in his tablets with a stylus the date, 'February 10, 1840'. On the same level with Cupid were black pedestals, raised at equal distances, flanking the royal group, and on them other Cupids displaying the heraldic ensigns of England, Scotland, and Ireland, and supporting large medallions upon fantastic shields, with the initials 'V.A.'; the frieze of each pedestal was beautifully ornamented with arabesques, the lower one with alternate wreaths and Cupids in relief, the wreaths surrounding the letters V.A. Upon the plateau of the cake were bands and festoons of orange blossom and myrtle entwined with roses, and sprigs of the same were placed loose, one to be given with each slice of the cake. A full border of orange blossoms, roses, and myrtle, was tastefully arranged round the lower portion, and the whole rested on a crimson velvet cloth.*
>
> ~FROM *ANECDOTES, PERSONAL TRAITS AND CHARACTERISTIC SKETCHES OF VICTORIA THE FIRST*, BY 'A LADY', 1840

Mawditt continued to make inventive and elaborate birthday, christening and Christmas cakes for the royal family into the 1840s.

....
Opposite: Cake made for the wedding of Victoria and Albert, 1840.

After looking about our rooms for a little while, I went and changed my gown, and then came back to his small sitting room where dearest Albert was sitting and playing; he had put on his Windsor coat; he took me on his knee, and kissed me and was so dear and kind. We had our dinner in our sitting room; but I had such a sick headache that I could eat nothing, and was obliged to lie down in the middle blue room for the remainder of the evening, on the sofa; but, ill or not, I never, never spent such an evening!! My dearest dearest dear Albert sat on a footstool by my side, and his excessive love and affection gave me feelings of heavenly love and happiness, I never could have hoped to have felt before! He clasped me in his arms, and we kissed each other again and again! His beauty, his sweetness and gentleness, – really how can I ever be thankful enough to have such a Husband! – At ½ p. 10 I went and undressed and was very sick, and at 20 m. p. 10 we both went to bed; (of course in one bed), to lie by his side, and in his arms, and on his dear bosom, and be called by names of tenderness, I have never yet heard used to me before – was bliss beyond belief! Oh! this was the happiest day of my life! – May God help me to do my duty as I ought and be worthy of such blessings!

VICTORIA'S JOURNAL, 10 FEBRUARY 1840

J UST BEFORE LEAVING for her brief three-day honeymoon at Windsor, Victoria took her leave of Lord Melbourne. They spent ten minutes together. 'Nothing could have gone off better,' he told her, with regard to the wedding ceremony. Victoria was greatly touched by the level of public rejoicing; that, he assured her, was because the people knew that the marriage 'is not for mere State reasons'. Lord M seemed tired and even more melancholy than usual. 'God bless you, Ma'am,' he said before Victoria and Albert left for Windsor, knowing that the period of exclusive and intense intimacy he had enjoyed with Victoria was now over for ever.

That sense of disengagement from the two people closest to her up until this point is reflected in the Queen's own words in her journal: 'We took leave of Mamma and drove off near 4; I and Albert alone.' But the placement of herself – as Queen – before Albert would not last for long. Within three months Albert was complaining of playing second fiddle: 'I am only the husband, and not the master in the house,' he told Victoria. It marked the onset of a battle of wills that would soon see his desk placed alongside hers and a shift from 'I' to 'we'.

A LTHOUGH THE QUEEN's journals were later carefully redacted by her daughter Beatrice after her death, enough of Victoria's joy at being married is clear for all to see in what survives of her account of her wedding night.

ALBERT:
Understand that all the things I asked for were so that I could have something of my own – my own position, my own freedom. The chance to do some good.

T HE FOLLOWING MORNING Victoria and Albert were, much
to everyone's surprise, up and taking the morning air on the
terrace at 8.30 a.m. She could barely tear herself away from Albert
long enough to dash off a hasty note to Melbourne saying it had
been a 'most gratifying and bewildering night' and an ecstatic letter
to Uncle Leopold that she was 'the happiest, happiest Being that ever
existed'. Albert was 'an Angel'; his kindness and affection was 'really
touching. To look into those dear eyes, and that dear sunny face,
is enough to make me adore him,' she avowed.

Six days after her wedding, Victoria sat down as usual to write
her diary. As she came to the last page of yet another leather-bound
volume, she paused to note this:

> *Here ends my twenty-eighth journal book, which contains the most
> interesting and the happiest time of my life.*
> ~VICTORIA'S JOURNAL, 16 FEBRUARY 1840

EMMA PORTMAN:
I don't think I have ever
seen a happier bride.
I believe she really
loves him.

❈❈

MELBOURNE:
I believe she does.

I T DOES NOT require much reading between the lines to deduce that, fortunately for Victoria, her lustful Hanoverian ancestors had passed down to her an enjoyment of the flesh rather than a crippling fear of it, for she seems to have embraced her life as a sexually fulfilled woman with relish. The last thing she therefore wanted so soon after marrying and discovering the pleasures of the marriage bed was to fall pregnant. But in the days before sex education and any really effective methods of contraception, there was little that she as an inexperienced bride could do to avoid it.

In conversation with Lord M back in December 1839, he had told her that 'the measure of married happiness is to have a great number of children'. Victoria had recoiled in horror, saying that that was 'the only thing I dread'. In later years she wrote of how she had hoped and prayed that she be spared 'this trial' so soon. 'If I had had a year of happy enjoyment with dear Papa, to myself – how thankful I should have been.' Instead, and much to her dismay, 'I was in for it at once – and furious I was.'

It would appear that Victoria fell pregnant within a month of her wedding and although Palace protocol allowed for no announcement, and a stony silence on her condition was maintained, everybody was watching for the tell-tale signs.

The first inklings came in the gossip columns when attention was drawn to the fact that the Queen had stopped riding out on horseback (on Dr Clark's orders). 'This was an indication,' wrote *The Morning Post*, 'of a state of health which at once led to the conclusion that a "nation's hopes" were in progress towards consummation.' The contemporary press had a fine time of it, concocting suitably respectful innuendo such as this.

A T A BALL not long after, it was noted that the Queen had been permitted 'to dance very little and to take her steps with great circumspection'. At the final Drawing Room of the season she had remained seated rather than standing to receive her guests. Eagle-eyed ladies present noted a widening in the royal waist and a heaviness in the figure. It was therefore concluded that the Queen was in 'that condition in which Ladies wish to be, who love their Lords'. The Dublin newspaper *Freeman's Journal* put it rather more bluntly on 25 March, when it revealed that the word from someone who had attended a recent Levée was that 'appearances FULLY indicate, that Her Majesty is in a fair way of perpetuating the Brunswick [i.e. Hanoverian] line in direct succession'.

Official news of the royal pregnancy was finally revealed four days after the attack by Edward Oxford, when *Bell's New Weekly Messenger* on 14 June ran the headline 'The Queen Enceinte' – even a rag such as *Bell's* adhering to the coy convention then in practice for using the French word *enceinte* for pregnant:

> *The event to which her Majesty and her people look forward with delight, not unmixed with anxiety, has become the subject of general conversation. It is even confidently said that some of the preparations have been settled, and that to Dr Locock, the eminent accoucheur (whose professional services were rendered to the Duchess of Sutherland under similar circumstances), has been entrusted with the important responsibility of watching over her Majesty's health, and of attending her on the interesting occasion.*
>
> ~ BELL'S NEW WEEKLY MESSENGER, 14 JUNE 1840

O XFORD'S ATTACK HAD also added fuel to the urgent need for Parliament to appoint a Regent, should the Queen be assassinated or die in childbirth. Victoria herself made it known that in the event of her death she wished Albert to act as Regent, much as her Uncle Leopold had been nominated during the pregnancy of Charlotte, Princess of Wales.

DUCHESS:
Who will care for you
by the side of the road?
One in three women
with child die, Drina.
One in three.

BEHIND THE SCENES, Prince Albert's former tutor and advisor Baron Stockmar had also been quietly working away for a Sole Regency for his protégé from the minute Victoria's pregnancy was known, in an attempt to defuse any humiliating debates in Parliament like those about Albert's personal allowance. Stockmar had therefore opened up discussion with Sir Robert Peel and Wellington to ensure this did not happen and that 'the Regent could and ought to be nobody but the prince'. The passing of the Regency Bill on 16 July was an important moment for Albert, at a time when he was still finding his feet. He wrote in triumph to his brother Ernest: 'I am to be Regent – alone – Regent, without a Council.'

The following day, the *London Gazette* confirmed Dr Charles Locock's appointment as Physician-Accoucheur, with two additional doctors: Robert Ferguson as 2nd Physician and Richard Blagden as Surgeon-Accoucheur. From now on, Victoria's advancing pregnancy would, necessarily, take her into increasing retreat. Pregnant queens did not parade themselves in public. As for when the child was due, that too was a guessing game, with the gossips talking of the Queen's 'confinement' being due in the first week of December.

HOWEVER, AT ABOUT 9 p.m. on 20 November, Victoria went into labour 'some days sooner than anticipated'. A monthly nurse, Mrs Mary Lilly, had already been appointed, on the recommendation of the Duchess of Sutherland, to look after her before and after the birth, and Dr Locock was summonsed.

The newspapers were desperate for any small detail about the birth of the Queen's first child; one later claimed, through good connections at court, that during her labour 'her Majesty evinced a firmness and composure almost incredible – at intervals exhibiting a cheerfulness and patient submission to her sufferings, in all respects consistent with the well-known attributes of her character'. Prince Albert's conduct was apparently exemplary and was 'distinguished by the most affectionate solicitude, combined with firmness'. At 1.50 a.m on the morning of 21 November a little girl, the Princess Royal, was born.

I N LINE WITH tradition, a group of VIPs had assembled in a connecting chamber: the Duchess of Kent, the Archbishop of Canterbury, the Bishop of London, the Lord Chancellor, Lord Melbourne, and other senior lords and Privy Councillors, 'whose constitutional duty it was to be present at the birth of an heir to the Throne'. They all gathered round expectantly as the baby's monthly nurse, Mrs Pegley,

> *...entered the room [...] with the 'young stranger', a beautiful, plump, and healthful Princess, wrapped in flannel, in her arms [...] Her Royal Highness was for a moment laid upon the table for the observation of the assembled authorities; but the loud tones in which she indicated her displeasure at such an exposure, while they proved the soundness of her lungs and the maturity of her frame, rendered it advisable that she should be returned to her chamber to receive her first attire.*
>
> ~ THE CUMBERLAND PACQUET, 1 DECEMBER 1840

This was virtually the only anecdote about the royal birth that made it to the British press. On running a banner headline 'Accouchement of the Queen' on 28 November, the *Standard* complained that it had:

> *...used every possible exertion to obtain any intelligence, however trivial, on so important and interesting an event, but the most profound silence reigns at the palace. The servants have instructions not to give the least information on the subject, or to answer any inquiry, from whatever quarter it may come.*
>
> ~ THE STANDARD, 28 NOVEMBER 1840

It is a tradition that is maintained to this day.

Although the child that Victoria had given birth to was three weeks early, she was large and healthy. But she was 'alas! a girl and not a boy, as we both had so hoped and wished for'. Victoria did not disguise her disappointment, but she was not one to be discouraged for long. 'Never mind,' she told Dr Locock, 'the next will be a Prince.'

THE ROYAL WET NURSE

T HE APPOINTMENT OF a wet nurse for Victoria's children was undertaken with extreme discretion, such appointments being made strictly by private arrangement and personal introduction or invitation. The wet nurse hired by Victoria for the Princess Royal (and we only know the names of three of those hired for her nine children) was Mrs Jane Ratsey, wife of a sailmaker of Cowes on the Isle of Wight. Her own baby, Restella Jane, had been born on 25 October 1840, one month before the Princess Royal.

According to the *Windsor and Eton Express*:

> *A Royal messenger was sent off express […] to Mr Charles Day, surgeon, of Cowes, to announce to Mrs Jane Ratsey, wife of Mr Restell Ratsey, of Medina Terrace, West Cowes, that she had been appointed wet-nurse to the Queen and to desire that she would proceed to London immediately […] A person apparently more admirably suited for the situation could not possibly have been selected […] It was her Majesty's particular wish that a wet-nurse should be chosen from the vicinity of Cowes, from observing the very healthy state of the women and children during her residence in the Isle of Wight, and from the very great benefit her own health received from her visits to that beautiful island.*

~ WINDSOR AND ETON EXPRESS, 28 NOVEMBER 1840

Right: The royal family in 1846.

I am taking up my Journal again, which was interrupted by my confinement, and am writing, as well as I can, from memory and short notes. – Just before the early hours of the morning of the 21st. I felt very uncomfortable and with difficulty aroused Albert from his sleep, who after a while, got Clark sent for. He came at 12 p. 2, Albert bringing him into the Bedroom. Clark said he would go to Locock. Tried to get to sleep again, but by 4, I got very bad and both the Doctors arrived. My beloved Albert was so dear and kind. Locock said the Baby was on the way and everything was all right. We both expressed joy that the event was at hand, and I did not feel at all nervous. After a good many hours suffering, a perfect little child was born at 2 in the afternoon, but alas! a girl and not a boy, as we both had so hoped and wished for. We were, I am afraid, sadly disappointed, but yet our hearts were full of gratitude, for God having brought me safely through my ordeal, and having such a strong, healthy child. Dearest Albert hardly left me at all, and was the greatest support and comfort. When he went to see Ministers, and the Baby was taken by Mrs Pegley (the monthly nurse for the Baby) into the room in which they were assembled, I saw good Lehzen for a moment. Dear Mama also came and was much relieved and delighted. – Albert had a late, hurried luncheon, and went to the Council at 4. I felt quite well and without a pain of any kind. Had some food and then, a good long sleep. – I awoke on the 22nd, having slept admirably and felt as well as if nothing had happened. Had an excellent appetite. Mama came to me for a little while and I also saw Lehzen and Stockmar for a moment. The dear little Baby was brought in to me several times and she was seen by numbers of people, Albert showing her. – The next days passed quietly and comfortably in the same way, and gradually I was allowed to do a little more. I have got a Wet Nurse for the Baby, a Mrs Ratsey, a fine young woman, wife of a sailmaker at Cowes, Isle of Wight.

BEHIND THE SCENES

WHENEVER WE, AS VIEWERS, tune into a new historical drama on television, it is usually the visuals – the sets, costumes and locations – that first attract our attention. But before any new drama goes into production there has to be a script; and before that script is even written, there needs to be a point of connection between the subject and the person who moulds that story for the screen.

In the case of *Victoria,* a female screenwriter has provided that crucial connection. As a woman and a mother, Daisy Goodwin's desire to turn Queen Victoria's young life into TV drama sprang from her own relationship with her youngest daughter.

In 2015 Daisy had been working on her third novel, about life at the court of Queen Victoria, when, not long into her research, she began to realise that despite all that had been written about her, there were still gaps in our knowledge of Victoria, particularly about her first years as a very young queen. Reading her vivid and detailed diaries it seemed obvious to Daisy that the personality of the volatile, feisty, teenage Victoria was the stuff of drama. That feeling was brought home to her, when, as Daisy recalls:

I had a fight with my teenage daughter, who like Victoria is small but mighty, and I found myself wondering what it would be like if overnight she became the most powerful woman in the world. This is, of course, what happened to the 18-year-old Victoria in 1837 when her uncle died. I couldn't get the idea of the teenage queen out of my head.

~DAISY GOODWIN, SCREENWRITER

I T WAS BY GETTING into the teenage mind of Victoria that Daisy realised she could access a new and revealing perspective on her life and her transition from princess to queen. Although she had worked in television as a documentary producer for years, this would be her first attempt at writing drama. For Daisy, good TV drama is all about exploring relationships, of presenting the emotional truth of a story, and to do this a screenwriter needs enough screen time to really engage the viewer with his or her characters. She wanted in particular to take the time to develop Victoria's relationships with those closest to her – Melbourne, Albert, her mother – over a longer time frame than is normally allowed in TV or film. It was Daisy's objective to portray:

> … a flawed young woman learning the hard way how to be queen […] to strip away the reverence that tends to stultify royalty on screen and show a young woman struggling with her responsibilities. Victoria was passionate and impulsive, and the first few years of her reign were full of blunders and mistakes.
>
> ~DAISY GOODWIN, SCREENWRITER

With this in mind, her initial treatment for a TV series was soon revised down to something much more personalised and intimate that would only cover the first four years of Victoria's reign. It allowed Daisy to focus in particular on Victoria's relationship with Lord Melbourne, which she feels is absolutely crucial to the story of her early years as queen:

> The biographies tend to gloss over the intensity of their friendship […] but if you read her diaries, which were redacted by her youngest daughter after her death, it's clear even from the passages that survive that the teenage monarch had a massive crush on the charming 'Lord M', as she called him.
>
> ~DAISY GOODWIN, SCREENWRITER

FOR THE FIRST TIME in any dramatisation of Victoria's life, Daisy's scripts really get under the skin of Victoria's relationship with Melbourne. The production has also been blessed with perfect casting which is shown in the marvellously sensitive and subtle performances of Jenna, and of Rufus Sewell as Melbourne. Jenna Coleman, right from the start was at the top of the list to play Victoria. Queen Victoria was only about 4 ft 11 in and it needed someone petite to convey her smallness, her vulnerability, but also her tremendous passion. The fascinating dynamic between Victoria and Melbourne, plus the growing and changing relationship between Albert and Victoria, leaves open the possibility to trace further along Victoria's gripping life story for a potential second series.

Beyond Daisy's challenge of creating the scripts for *Victoria*, the production company, Mammoth Screen, faced its own, equally big challenge in recreating the world of 1830s England. More specifically, the biggest logistical challenge was finding a substitute for the key location for the story – Buckingham Palace – where it was, of course, impossible to film.

We could have found a stately home, or several, and tried to make those look like the Palace, but shooting on location in stately homes is notoriously difficult. So I had it in my mind that we might have to build a set. You need to get control, which you do by building a set, and you can shoot a higher page count per day, generally, than you can on location. You have to make room in the schedule for big set pieces such as weddings, where you may only get a minute's worth of material in a day. ~PAUL FRIFT, SERIES PRODUCER

Driving through the gates of Leeds East airport, in the tiny Yorkshire village of Church Fenton, you couldn't feel further away from the splendour of Buckingham Palace. As well as the two huge hangars, the former RAF base has a working airstrip flanked by grey one-storey buildings, a car park and a rickety-looking control tower. But just through the door of hangar no. 1 lies a sumptuous surprise that will transport viewers back in time to the opulent corridors, bedrooms and drawing rooms of a royal palace in 1837.

The Buckingham Palace set is the brainchild of designer Michael Howells, whose previous work includes films such as *Nanny McPhee*, *Bright Young Things* and *Emma*.

If you're going to build Buckingham Palace as a set, you need an extraordinary designer and that's what we've got in Michael. He is not just experienced in feature films and TV, but also in theatre, and he even organises parties for the very rich, so he brought all that to bear on what we were doing and the result is astounding.
~PAUL FRIFT, SERIES PRODUCER

MICHAEL STARTED WORK on the design for *Victoria* in the summer of 2015 and, after seven weeks of planning, the set was up and ready for filming over an 11-week schedule. 'Admittedly we were still banging up paintings in some of the rooms after shooting started,' revealed supervising art director Fabrice Spelta, who was Michael's right-hand man on the build. 'But we got there in the end.'

❧ ❧ ❧

ALTHOUGH THERE are no records or photographs of the Royal Apartments inside Buckingham Palace in 1837, the lavish décor recreated for the series was authentic for the period down to the last detail. Georgian wallpapers were reproduced and the carpets specially made and printed with a period design. The gold chairs and liberally gilded tables dotted throughout the rooms were made to order and then hand-lacquered on site, and the paintings produced by the art team.

We needed a lot of paintings for the palace and that can prove expensive. So for the portraits, including King George III and Victoria's father, the Duke of Kent, we got prints from the Royal collection, had them blown up and then we made the frames.

~MICHAEL HOWELLS, PRODUCTION DESIGNER

Queen Victoria came to the throne long before electric lighting, and gas lighting had only been installed as a try-out in a few parts of the Palace, so the rooms were almost entirely lit by candles:

We estimated that we would use 400 a day but we ended up using 900 on some days and ordered them by the 1,000 from an amazing man in Cumbria, who makes them by hand. We had to have someone on fire watch the whole time, in case the place went up, because there were so many candles, especially when we did the big ball scenes.

~MICHAEL HOWELLS, PRODUCTION DESIGNER

ICTORIA'S TEAL BLUE and silver bedroom in the show is dominated by a huge four-poster bed on a raised platform with sumptuous embroidered drapes around its dark wood pillars. A small upholstered sofa sits in the centre, and four tiny chairs, arranged in a row, provide seats for four of the dolls that Victoria was so fond of, even into her adulthood.

A lot of the ornaments were rented, but we also bought a lot, so we went to a lot of auctions to find beautiful Georgian pieces, like beautiful dark wood cabinets in the bedroom. The bed was brought in from the Czech Republic.

~MICHAEL HOWELLS, PRODUCTION DESIGNER

The wallpaper was copied from an 1809 design and the wall panels created through a process called *verre églomisé*, meaning gilded glass, and real silver leaf was used to create an authentic sheen around the room.

The windows were hung with Chinese silk drapes. 'They looked luxurious but this is really cheap silk from China,' said Michael. 'We have one very clever lady who made all the curtains and drapes for the whole set and she did it all in nine weeks.'

HE HIGH CEILING in Victoria's drawing room in the show is lit by huge chandeliers holding hundreds of candles. 'They are double chandeliers,' said designer Michael Howells. 'We took one chandelier and stuck it to the top of another one because they weren't big enough as they were. These are electric, lit with candle bulbs, but they would have been real candles in Victoria's day.'

The room is lined with paintings, huge vases sit on enormous gold corbels (the elaborate carved brackets that hold ornaments) and imposing pillars add a majestic note to the architecture. But the opulence of the gold fixtures and fittings, and the marble pillars, was deceiving.

'The pillars were cardboard, rolled into a column and then marbled,' Michael continued. While the roundel in the impressive coat of arms above the door 'was a shield from a child's suit of armour I bought in a pound shop, which was covered in gold leaf'.

FRANCATELLI'S KITCHEN

 S CELEBRATED CHEF FRANCATELLI, actor Ferdinand Kingsley got to try out his culinary skills in the kitchens – with a little professional help.

I'm a pretty decent cook but it's a very different set-up in an amazing old kitchen like the one at Harewood. My own cooking skills only stood the test for about 30 seconds at a time, between action and cut. We made bacon, peas and mint for the Queen, which is one of [Francatelli's] recipes, and we did a lot of amazing confectionery, because he was an incredible chocolatier and pastry maker.

We did a lot of amazing chocolate, including a whole pineapple dipped in chocolate, chocolate bombes and melted down chocolate for hot chocolate. There was also some ornate icing – which I had a little bit of help with – piping Victoria and Albert's initials, and lots of gold leafing. The art department was amazing and we had a brilliant home economist, who made sure that it all looked authentic. But no one was going to eat anything I made, especially anything that was meat that I was doing over and over again. That would have killed you!

~FERDINAND KINGSLEY, WHO PLAYS FRANCATELLI

CASTLES AND HOUSES

RABY CASTLE

BUILT IN THE FOURTEENTH century and set in 200 acres of deer park, Raby Castle was chosen as the fictional Chillingham Hall, where Victoria and Albert visit one of the oldest seats in the country.

Raby Castle was our star attraction, where we had to go out of our comfort zone distance wise. The land was first owned by King Canute so it's old money and it shows.

~JIM ALLAN, LOCATIONS MANAGER

BRAMHAM PARK

MANY OF THE OUTDOOR scenes set at Windsor, either on horseback or in coach and horses, were filmed at Bramham Park, near Leeds, which sits in 200 acres of landscaped grounds. 'There was a track leading up to the front of the house, lined by an avenue of trees, which was perfect,' said Jim Allan. 'So we shot there and the Milk team generated Windsor Castle at the end, instead of Bramham. For the actual Great Park, you can use any park and woodland because you don't see the castle.'

WENTWORTH WOODHOUSE

THIS EIGHTEENTH-CENTURY PILE near Rotherham has the longest country house façade in Europe, at 606 feet, and boasts over 3,000 rooms and a footprint that covers more than 2.5 acres. This immense stately home stood in for the Duke of Cumberland's house, and the pillared hall was used for a fencing sequence with Albert. The old stable-yards also became the grimy Dickensian streets of the East End.

ALLERTON CASTLE

THE AUSTERE AND IMPOSING surroundings of the German castles, which Albert, Ernest and Leopold called home back in Saxe-Coburg, was provided by the splendour of this North Yorkshire house. Built in the 1850s by architect George Martin, in the Tudor-Gothic style, it was restored to its former glory in 2005, after a fire destroyed much of the north wing of the house.

**ALEX JENNINGS, WHO PLAYS
KING LEOPOLD**
'Some of my scenes were set in the
castle in Germany, the family seat,
which was actually Allerton Castle
in Yorkshire. It was brilliantly chosen,
a huge gothic pile. They stuffed it full
of antlers and stuffed animals and it
looked incredibly authentic. That really
helped me get into the character and
his background.'

QUEEN VICTORIA'S ACCESSION to the throne marked the beginning of a new era in both her personal style and the fashion of the nation. The Regency era, with its Empire line dresses and lightweight fabrics, had already given way to a fuller skirt, high waists and puffed sleeves, but, when Victoria became Queen, the style changed again.

Towards the 1840s, the huge puffed sleeves disappeared, the waist came back down and the conical skirt was replaced by a bell-shaped skirt. Skirts started to get bigger and bigger and they had petticoats with more and more frills, which got so heavy women could hardly walk. Eventually the crinoline frame came in, to take the weight and hold the skirts up, because the weight was dragging them down. It was a really repressive era for women, fashion-wise. They had corsets, heavy petticoats, sleeves which were so tight they could hardly move their arms, and bonnets with veils so they could barely see.

~ROSALIND EBBUTT, COSTUME DESIGNER

The transition is even more marked in Victoria herself, whose new role as Queen meant that, at eighteen, she had to grow up almost overnight.

Victoria starts the series with more childlike dresses, with big sleeves. So she's dressed like that as a young queen when she first comes to the throne, as an eager young girl. But then her style moves on as she becomes more mature, so the waistline goes down and the sleeve shape changes as she becomes a woman, a wife and a mother. That's been very useful in illustrating the transition from Victoria as a child to a more mature young woman, and we were able to follow that path with the changes in style.

~ROSALIND EBBUTT, COSTUME DESIGNER

WITH OVER 30 PRINCIPAL members of cast and numerous ladies in waiting, downstairs staff, visiting diplomats and politicians, plus hundreds of extras for the bigger scenes, Rosalind and her small team of six had their work cut out. In order to dress everyone, she used a combination of making clothes from scratch, having items made to order and hiring from three main costumiers.

For Victoria's wardrobe, I would say about three-quarters was new and a quarter found, hired or bought. I went to the fabric shops in Shepherd's Bush, London, and I found all the fabric I needed for the Queen's dresses, so that we could have them made. Some people's costumes are entirely new and others have had a few things made.

~ROSALIND EBBUTT, COSTUME DESIGNER

The men's formal dress jackets, which are military-style with heavy gold embroidery, were hired from specialists because of the huge cost of making them new. At Windsor, for example, the full dress livery that Albert wore was a very dark navy coat with heavy gold embroidery around the collars and cuffs and along the front panels.

The costumiers took the bits of a livery and then sewed them on to a new coat, so we didn't have to pay for the gold trimming, which costs thousands. If you look closely at the embroidery, it is not thread but a very fine gold wire with a thread going through it so it's like a very tight gold spring. Were we to have made a new one, it would have cost £10,000. And it weighs a ton!

~ROSALIND EBBUTT, COSTUME DESIGNER

TOM HUGHES, WHO PLAYS PRINCE ALBERT

'The costumes were beautiful. A lot of them were custom made so they fitted perfectly and naturally held you in position.

The coats were incredibly heavy but that was quite helpful because we were filming in a big aircraft hangar in Yorkshire and it could get pretty cold. Having a big thick heavy wool jacket was very helpful. After all, I was not the one with my shoulders out wearing a corset so I didn't dare complain about my costume.

The wedding jacket was the heaviest, partly because of the gold chain and all the other add-ons. But I'm not someone who can act with my phone in my pocket, I have to have the correct things for the role so it's great that the costume felt as it would have felt, that it was made out of the material it would have been made from. Plus it was a good workout!'

ONCE THEY HAD BEEN worn, the costumes could also be recycled into completely different outfits for other scenes. For the wedding, for example, Rosalind had eight cream bridesmaids dresses made from a design Victoria herself sketched in her journal. But once the nuptials were over, they were given a new lease of life:

We kept four as they were, and I then had some dyed and re-trimmed so we could use them as evening dresses. I found this beautiful rich burgundy lace at a shop in Shepherd's Bush, then I sent the dresses to be dyed and told them these four dresses needed to go with this lace so they came up with pinks and the dresses are completely unrecognisable.

~ROSALIND EBBUTT, COSTUME DESIGNER

The female cast members wore corsets under their long dresses as well as a quilted petticoat which, according to Rosalind, was much lighter than the real thing.

The costumes were quite cumbersome but very beautiful. The padded petticoats were literally like a duvet but we were quite thankful for that because it was very cold when we were filming. They were fabulous costumes. Both James Keast and Ros have got a beautiful eye for colour but also they did so much research and the materials were extraordinary. The texture and the colours were like nothing you would ever see in a shop nowadays. It felt like such a privilege to wear them.

~ANNA WILSON-JONES, WHO PLAYS EMMA PORTMAN

FOR BIG STATE OCCASIONS, costume designer Rosalind Ebbutt referenced many contemporary paintings by royal artists, including George Hayter and Franz Xaver Winterhalter. For the wedding in 1840 there was a vivid description of the Queen's dress, and sketches that Victoria drew in her journal of her veil and her headdress. The actual dress survives and is on show in Kensington Palace, along with the military jacket Albert wore, but, as Rosalind explained, these were less helpful than one might imagine.

> *The wedding dress that still exists has been altered, because they took the lace off and altered other parts. Albert's coat is also in Kensington Palace but it is nothing like what he actually wore because, after he died, Queen Victoria had embroidered embellishments put on it, saying 'My beloved Albert' and things like that so it doesn't look at all like the original any more.*
>
> *We made the veil, which she sketched in her diary, out of old lace and it was pinned in her hair. She didn't have it over her face. Then we had an orange blossom headdress made for her hair.*
>
> ~ROSALIND EBBUTT, COSTUME DESIGNER

Victoria's train, which required eight bridesmaids to carry it, was also reproduced with 24 feet of creamy white silk satin, protected on the underside with curtain liner, and decorated with an intricate floral design around the edges.

Tom Hughes, who plays Albert, wore a red field marshal's jacket with genuine gold epaulettes and more of that gold lace embroidery. As Victoria's husband he automatically became a member of the Order of the Garter, so the Queen ordered a special wedding gift for him.

> *Victoria had an embroidered diamond garter made for him as well as a garter chain. For herself, she had an extra-long diamond garter chain made in special lightweight gold so it wouldn't drag her dress down, so we had a replica made. The garter traditionally went round the knee, but Queen Victoria was the first woman to be elevated to the Order of the Garter and she couldn't wear it on her leg because it wouldn't be visible. So she had a special one made that buckled around her arm, over her sleeve.*
>
> ~ROSALIND EBBUTT, COSTUME DESIGNER

I N LINE WITH THE changing fashions of the day, the arrival of Victoria ushered in new trends in hair and make-up. Styles before her reign began were as elaborate and flamboyant as possible, with plaits, braids and buns piled up on the top of the head, ringlets cascading down on either side, and huge decorations placed in the hair for even more dramatic effect. Stylist Nic Collins explained:

> There was a style called the Coiffure '37, which was in vogue at the time. The women were all wearing hugely ostentatious styles with exaggerated knots – Apollo knots – piled high on top of the head. So at the start of the series, when Victoria attends a ball, everybody, even the extras, had these huge hairstyles with exaggerated knots, curls and ringlets. When Victoria came in she was all for simplicity, so she wanted a very simple hairstyle. All the hair came down, everything came down the head, and the new look was a centre parting with dropped buns or plaits at the side.
>
> ~NIC COLLINS, STYLIST

For Nic and her team, the earlier, more flamboyant styles meant more research and learning new techniques. For big events, like the ball scene, it also involved creating up to 200 incredible hairstyles in a day. 'We had great fun recreating the styles of the past,' she said.

> We found a picture of Louise Lehzen where she had hair woven like a basket so we gave the character the same style, created in exactly the same way. It took a whole day to work out how to basket weave with hair and how to make it so someone could wear that, on set, for a whole day when they don't have the actual hair to do it with.
>
> ~NIC COLLINS, STYLIST

As the lead, and the most recognisable character, it was crucial that Jenna looked as close to the real Queen Victoria as possible. Her stint in the hair and make-up truck, which sits alongside the set, was the longest at an hour 15 minutes. As she had shoulder-length hair, extensions were woven into her real hair, so that it could be styled in the loose buns favoured by the Queen, or left loose for the more informal scenes in her boudoir. Her make-up was then applied to look as natural as possible, to tie in with the simple unadorned fashion of the period.

> *Wigs had become a bit of a no-no because of the tax, which meant they were phased out. The only people who wore wigs were liveried servants, clergy and judges but in a document from 1840, only 900 servants were registered to wear wigs and if you imagine that one house could have up to 900 staff, that's not a huge number.*
>
> ~NIC COLLINS, STYLIST

At Kensington Palace, with Sir John Conroy controlling the purse strings, wigs were discarded, but with the Queen's accession, when the household staff moved to Buckingham Palace, that changed.

> *The staff who came from Kensington to Buckingham Palace now had to wear them, which Penge hates. Although he had one in Kensington he didn't wear it so we had two types of wig – the old shoddy wigs and the grander, clean-cut livery wig he gets at the Palace.*
>
> ~NIC COLLINS, STYLIST

The wigs cost up to £4,000 each, and in order to keep them pristine, the hair and make-up truck featured an unusual appliance – a wig oven. The hair was wrapped around wooden rollers and baked in the heated metal box to set the style. 'The wig oven stopped the style dropping out,' explained Nic. 'Without that we wouldn't have got 12 hours of wear from them on set.'

CAST LIST

Jenna Coleman – Victoria

Rufus Sewell – Lord Melbourne

Tom Hughes – Prince Albert

Catherine H. Flemming – Duchess of Kent

Daniela Holtz – Baroness Louise Lehzen

Paul Rhys – Sir John Conroy

Adrian Schiller – Penge

Tommy Lawrence Knight – Brodie

Eve Myles – Mrs Jenkins

Nell Hudson – Miss Skerrett

Margaret Clunie – Duchess of Sutherland

Anna Wilson-Jones – Lady Emma Portman

Peter Firth – Duke of Cumberland

Nichola McAuliffe – Duchess of Cumberland

Peter Bowles – Duke of Wellington

Nigel Lindsay – Sir Robert Peel

Robin McCallum – Lord Portman

Pete Ivatts – Archbishop of Canterbury

Alice Orr-Ewing – Lady Flora Hastings

Tom Price – Duke of Sutherland

Alex Jennings – Leopold

David Oakes – Prince Ernest

Jordan Waller – Lord Alfred Paget

Andrew Bicknell – Duke of Coburg

Nicholas Agnew – Prince George

Ferdinand Kingsley – Charles Francatelli

Basil Eidenbenz – Lohlein

Daniel Donskoy – Grand Duke Alexander Nikolaevich

Robin Soans – Sir James Clark

Guy Oliver Watts – Sir George Hayter

Nicholas Agnew – Prince George

Julian Finnigan – Lord Hastings

Richard Dixon – Lord Chancellor

Simon Paisley Day – Lord Chamberlain

Andrew Bicknell – Duke of Coburg

David Bamber – Duke of Sussex

Claire Willie – Lady Peel

Ben Abell – Rowland Hill

Samantha Colley – Eliza

James Wilby – Sir Piers Giffard

Harry McEntire – Edward Oxford

Andrew Scarborough – Captain Childers

Annabel Mullion – Lady Beatrice

PICTURE CREDITS

HarperCollins*Publishers*
1 London Bridge Street
London SE1 9GF
www.harpercollins.co.uk

First published by HarperCollins*Publishers* 2016

10 9 8 7 6 5 4 3 2 1

Text © Helen Rappaport 2016

A Mammoth Screen/Masterpiece Co-production for ITV
Television series, photographs and 'Victoria' logo © Mammoth Screen Limited 2016. All rights reserved.
Victoria series photography by Gareth Gatrell
Cover photography © Billy & Hells
All other images © see page 303
Design © Smith & Gilmore

All quotes featured in page margins are taken from the fictional *Victoria* television scripts written by Daisy Goodwin.
All interviews with cast and crew supplied by Alison Maloney, with the exception of p273–4.

Transcripts of Victoria's journals, containing all original stress and emphasis, can be found at
www.queenvictoriasjournals.org

With thanks to Patrick Smith

Helen Rappaport asserts the moral right to be identified as the author of this work

A catalogue record of this book is available from the British Library

Main hardback ISBN 978-0-00-819683-7
The Book People ISBN 978-0-00-795997-6

Printed and bound in Spain by Graficas Estella